Let My Spirit Soar!

Narratives of Diverse Women in School Leadership

Maenette K. P. Ah Nee-Benham
Joanne E. Cooper

CORWIN PRESS, INC.
A Sage Publications Company
Thousand Oaks, California

For information:

Corwin Press, Inc.
A Sage Publications Company
2455 Teller Road
Thousand Oaks, California 91320
E-mail: order@corwinpress.com

CORWIN
PRESS

SAGE Publications Ltd.
6 Bonhill Street
London EC2A 4PU
United Kingdom

SAGE Publications India Pvt. Ltd.
M-32 Market
Greater Kailash I
New Delhi 110 048 India

Printed in the United States of America

Library of Congress Cataloging-in-Publication Data

This book is printed on acid-free paper.

Ah Nee-Benham, Maenette K. P.
    Let my spirit soar: Narratives of diverse women in school leadership /
by Maenette K. P. Ah Nee-Benham & Joanne E. Cooper.
        p. cm.
    Includes bibliographical references.
    ISBN 0-8039-6671-7 (cloth: acid-free paper).
    ISBN 0-8039-6672-5 (pbk.: acid-free paper)
    1. Minority women educators—United States. 2. Minority women in the
professions—United States. 3. Educational leadership—United States.
4. Narration (Rhetoric) I. Cooper, Joanne E. II. Title.
    LB2831.62.A42 1997
    370′.89′00973—dc21   97-33952

98 99 00 01 02 03 10 9 8 7 6 5 4 3 2 1

Production Editor: Sherrise M. Purdum
Cover Designer: Marcia M. Rosenburg
Production Assistant: Karen Wiley
Editorial Assistant: Kristen L. Green
Typesetter/Designer: Marion Warren
Print Buyer: Anna Chin

Contents

Part 2: Concluding Thoughts

Foreword

This is a remarkable book, reporting individual stories of women who exemplify personal self-reliance and leadership in a variety of contexts. It is a courageous endeavor to demonstrate how women from diverse backgrounds and ancestry contribute to the schooling of youth. But it is also a book that presents living individuals situated in a history of human relationships who share their narratives that inspire reason for schooling.

One of the areas in school leadership most obviously neglected is minority women's leadership. Many reasons have been forwarded. This book presents minority women's leadership in a subtle and poetic way but, nevertheless, profound. Minority women relate their personal and private stories, and through their voices, the reader is afforded an unusual peek into qualities of leadership and into personal and professional attributes grounded in gender and ethnicity. The similarities between the minority women and others are acknowledged, but it is the differences and individual attributes as they determine how leadership is enacted that are valuable in this work.

Those who lose patience with slow changes in schools might benefit from examining how minority women conduct their private and public lives. It is these individuals who master skills of critique, adjustment, and framing of social interaction and action. Thus, the fundamental contribution of this work is establishing how minority status based on gender and ethnicity determines school leadership enactment. The authors, through the presentation of individual minority women's "voices," lay out the different profiles. As the mosaic of individual experiences develops, the reader is invited to contrast, compare, and evaluate on two dimensions: the personal differences and leadership characteristics each woman brings to the situation.

Nine women's stories are presented. Each story contains within it the nuances and complexities inherent in their gender and ethnic backgrounds as well as in the organizational positions they hold or have held. Tina, a Filipino woman, holds a district office administrative position. Yvonne, a Latina, Algonquin, and Italian woman; Catherine, of Cuban descent; and Sarah, a lesbian, hold elementary principalship positions in their respective school districts. Rachel, a Japanese American, serves as a vice principal of a suburban elementary school. Jolie, African American, wears different hats in her assignment: She is an inner-city middle-school department chair of the counseling department, counselor of the 8th-grade class, and summer school principal for the high school. Margaret, a Tamil Indian woman, and Jackie, an African American, are elementary teachers. Opal, of Chinese descent, is a retired teacher who had taught for 40 years in elementary schools. Each individual's story is poignant but hopeful, and each individual's leadership is toward the betterment of children's lives.

Researchers and others have asked, How do life experiences and personal attributes contribute to successful leadership? And how do particular social and cultural situations determine successful leadership? This book provides some insight and partial answers to these questions. Ethnic women, by virtue of their marginality, find useful ways to balance their home lives and professional lives. They learn to develop and establish webs of support, and they resist suppression and injustice through nonconfrontation. They may take a stand, but equally, silent determination may wear down an opponent. Their resistance is strengthened through a network of community relationships or the application of wit to maintain a balance.

The authors identify four themes that run through the lives of these women. The first refers to these women's understanding that they are different. This pervasive sense of difference calls for a collective voice and collective learning, which turns out to be the political challenge these women pose to others. The second theme—determination and courage—is reflected in their persistence and search for fairness as well as in their retention of optimism and goodwill. Regarding the third theme, the authors refer to these women's sense of compassion for children as a demonstration of the "public process of loving." Finally, the redefinition of power and authority is presented not only through the fact that these women are not holders of the traditional hierarchical posts of power, such as the superintendencies or high school principalships, but through the fact that they garner power through their relationships between equals. The authors describe this type of power as that which champions the moral aspects of equity and fairness in schooling. These women succeed through their silent but relentless efforts and highly developed interpersonal skills.

I applaud Maenette K. P. Ah Nee-Benham and Joanne Cooper for writing a book from which I learned and about which I reflected. It is my wish that my colleagues in the world of school improvement and reform will read this book and consider its lessons. Most important, I hope that the worlds of teaching, school administration, and school policy, now so divided by struggles over the purposes and functions of schooling and the growing diversity among the children in schools, will grasp the important insights and understandings of this presentation of personal narratives. It is through the appreciation of each person's composite of attitudes, skills, and knowledge that communities of understanding can be developed and leadership for the schooling of children can mostly effectively be enacted.

FLORA IDA ORTIZ
Professor, School of Education
University of California, Riverside

Preface

Much of the previous work on educational leadership has focused on traditional epistemologies, such as the "great man" theory, which have excluded the voices of women and minorities. As we move into the 21st century and the world of education becomes increasingly dedicated to issues of diversity and equity, new conceptions of leadership are needed. This book is one attempt to expand the leadership paradigm by examining conceptions of leadership from the margins, conceptions that reflect other cultures and societies than mainstream United States. It is these margins that we believe to be fertile ground for the transformation of educational leadership, a place where energized dedication to the creation of inclusive communities of learning can grow. It is our hope that the stories of the nine school leaders contained within these pages will expand current perspectives on leadership and explore the impact of culture and communities on those who lead.

This book contains the stories of nine diverse women school leaders. Each narrative is an exploration of a life in education, teaching children, leading teachers, forming communities of learners in the hope that all will be enhanced rather than diminished by the experiences they share.

The writing of each story is an affirmation of the power of collective and connective activities. Our first chapter asserts a particular need to study diverse ways of knowing and doing and provides a discussion of the use of narrative or story as a means of deep reflection and learning. This chapter is then followed by portraits of each woman as she journeys between and across multiple worlds. Each story is the collaborative effort of both researcher and participant as they weave together the threads of professional and personal experience. The final chapter brings to the surface themes of difference, determination, caring, and the redefining of power and authority that emerge from the stories and connects these insights to present concerns regarding teaching, learning, and school leadership. Finally, we link our dialogue to the politics of voice, which commits to a reflection of differences within the constructive activity of community building.

We, the authors, come to these stories as listeners, tellers, learners, and collectors of memories. Our role has been to elicit these personal and professional stories through long hours of listening and hours of observing each leader in her school setting. This study required extensive conversations with each woman—hours of taping, transcribing, and analysis of those transcripts—as well as the study of each woman's personal artifacts and journals. Through collaborative storymaking, we have constructed these narratives in conjunction with the storytellers, crafting together a mutually told tale of each woman's life and her understanding of educational leadership.

An increasing amount of research conducted by social and political scientists is beginning to address the issues of difference and inequity in substantive ways that reveal the struggles often faced by minority men and women in education. Nevertheless, we believe that it is instructive to examine deeply the *re*presentations of these stories to inform a broader readership, one that is open to exploring differences in perceptions and practices of school leadership. We believe that within these stories lie new answers to old problems, new ways of understanding the increasingly multicultural populations encountered in schools today.

At one level, this work sheds some light on the value of narrative as inherently linked to school leaders' ways of knowing and action (Bruner, 1986; Elbaz, 1990; Sarbin, 1986). On another level, the value of the minority voice is that it recognizes the different cultural, ethnic, and social backgrounds of educators, thereby revealing multiple perceptions and relationships between the school and the professionals within that school. In addition, the presentation of the minority voice, that of the participant and of the researcher-writer, within the context of a public forum, encourages more dialogue that is inclusive and affirming. The importance of sharing our stories is to emphasize the potential power of the narrative genre to assist re-searcher-writers, participant-tellers, and readers to rediscover and reacquaint themselves with their many personal and professional ways of knowing.

If we have had relatively little dialogue about the stories of "other" school leaders, it is at least partly due to an educational leadership discourse and practice that has been structured to impede such treatment. Here, the work of feminist scholars and cultural criti-cal theorists may provide more clarity (see Bloom & Munro, 1995). The intention of our approach is to encourage dialogue among dif-ferent perspectives and to examine the tensions of several texts that include the self versus the school's institutional governance norms as well as the professional self versus the personal and cultural self. In addition, our task here is to expand the meanings of different modes of experience and existence that both explore and contest es-tablished frames or ways of seeing. This work examines how these women's lives reveal ontological and political discourses and prac-tices that divert from mainstream thought and that present vari-ations on leadership themes in delightfully innovative and surpris-ing ways.

There is much we might learn from the stories of minority women school leaders, but stories remain only romantic interludes until examined. In this work, we hope to push the narrative, to trans-form the story into metaphor that can teach us how to think about and to address the problems of schools and learning in an increas-ingly multicultural society. The voices of the women, whose lives unfold within the covers of this book, are fresh and not simply ap-propriations of white European stories. The message transcends mere reactionary responses to domination. That is not to say that revealing oppression is unimportant but that its existence will pre-sent itself in subtle and startling ways throughout each story. What we may read beyond the printed text can teach us new ways of think-ing about education, ways that, as bell hooks (1994a) urges, "open our minds and hearts so that we can know beyond the boundaries of what is acceptable, so that we can think and rethink, so that we can create new visions—a movement against boundaries" (p. 12).

What follows, then, are the stories of nine minority women school leaders. These women are not the highly decorated exemplars held up by their school districts as the elite few who have made it in the system. In truth, we avoided the light of the ethnic minority celebrity as a text of true representation of the hardworking school leader. Not that our leaders are not hardworking, but we have never felt comfortable being manipulated by the system that chooses to identify "successful" school leaders as those who legitimize a hierarchical structure. Instead, the women we interviewed were recommended by professional practitioners, teachers, and school leaders with whom we have worked closely in classroom settings, graduate course work, and other field experiences. Many of these participants have not traded their integrity for conformity but instead reveal through their stories new ways of understanding school leadership, new ways of responding to the demands of educational systems steeped in traditional bureaucratic norms. Their stories are both enlightening and inspirational as the soaring of their spirits takes us to new heights of understanding.

Note: There are many groups who have been disenfranchised that we do not mention directly within the text of this work. However, we do submit that there is a need for more discourse regarding issues of race-ethnicity, gender, class, sexual orientation, physical and mental ableism, age, geography, and position.

Acknowledgments

Mahalo! To the women who gave their stories as gifts of learning. I know that the truths of each story will outlive our analysis of their content. It is not possible to acknowledge everyone who supported this effort, however, a special thank you to Cathy Robinson, the Institute for Research on Teaching at Michigan State University, and Gracia Alkema of Corwin Press. Mahalo nui loa! To our colleagues in K-12 schools, students and friends, helpers, caregivers, and healers.

Maenette

I would like to thank the wonderful school leaders who generously gave their time, energy and thoughtful responses to the questions we posed in collecting narratives for this book. Your careful review of your stories made them clearer, stronger accounts of your work and your lives. Thanks, too, for the strong role model I have in the woman who came before me, my loving mother, and the women who come after me, my two beautiful daughters. You have been inspirations to me in so many ways. The women of the Research on Women and Education Special Interest Group (SIG) of AERA have also been supportive and loving as I follow this professor path. Thank you for your wisdom and your laughter. Both have been invaluable. Without the SIG we would not have met Gracia Alkema, who has given us continuous and enthusiastic support as we moved steadily and swiftly toward publication. Thank you for your belief in our work.

Joanne

We gratefully acknowledge permission to reprint portions from the following:

Pat Mora, *Nepantla*, University of New Mexico Press, copyright 1993.
bell hooks, *Teaching to Transgress: Education as the Practice of Freedom*, Routledge, copyright 1994.
Maya Angelou, *Wouldn't Take Nothing for my Journey Now*, Random House Inc., copyright 1993.
Kahlil Gibran, *The Prophet*, Alfred A. Knopf, copyright 1923/1951.
Joy Harjo, "Transformations," from *In Mad Love and War*, copyright © 1990 by Joy Harjo, Wesleyan University Press by permission of University Press of New England.
Audre Lorde, "A Litany for Survival," from *The Black Unicorn* by Audre Lorde, copyright © 1978 by Audre Lorde. Reprinted by permission of W. W. Norton & Company, Inc.
Leslie Marmon Silko, *Ceremony*, by Leslie Marmon Silko. Copyright © 1977 by Leslie Silko. Used by permission of Viking Penguin, a division of Penguin Books USA Inc.

About the Authors

Maenette K. P. Ah Nee-Benham, Assistant Professor, Educational Administration, Michigan State University, is a Native Hawaiian teacher and scholar. She has taught grades kindergarten and 1, 3, and 4, and 7 through 12 and has held administrative positions in pre-kindergarten and K-12 (kindergarten through 12th grade) schools. Currently, she teaches a cross-cultural undergraduate course and graduate courses in school leadership, organizational theory, schools-families-community, school change, inquiry, and issues of diversity in school leadership. Her inquiry centers on the use of narrative to reveal issues and practices of school leadership, teaching and learning strategies that explore practitioner understanding and practice, and the effects of educational policy on native people. She is the author of numerous articles in each of these areas and has authored the book, *Culture and Educational Policy in Hawai'i: The Silencing of Native Voices.*

Joanne E. Cooper, Associate Professor, Educational Administration, University of Hawaii-Manoa, has worked as both teacher and administrator in K-12 public schools as well as in community colleges and 4-year universities. She holds degrees in elementary education, speech pathology, curriculum and instruction, and in educational policy and management. She currently teaches courses in organizational theory, organizational change, qualitative research, critical reflection in administration, adult learning, and curriculum in higher education. Her research examines the work of women and minorities in education, the use of narrative as both phenomenon and method, and the study of organizational change in education. She is the author of numerous articles and books in these areas and has most recently coauthored *The Constructivist Leader* and "Asian Women Leaders of Higher Education: Stories of Strength and Self-Discovery" in *Everyday Knowledge and Uncommon Truths: Life Writings and Women's Experiences In and Outside of the Academy.*

Dedication

In the corner of the window in the last stall of the women's bathroom on the second floor of the College of Education building is a small, bright red, foil origami crane. Not more than an inch across, it sits with its tiny wings spread and its neck tilted to one side. Next to it is a large, squarish chunk of gun metal gray lint. Behind it is a cobweb filled with flecks of black dirt strung throughout its expanse. The window is boarded over, this being a stall in a ladies' room, so the bright red crane seems to sing, the only happy note in its glum surroundings. It has been there for almost a year now, the gift of some talented and generous stranger. Everyone who sees and does not take it home leaves behind this same gift for the rest of us to enjoy again and again.

This crane is a symbol of our hope for women and minorities in education. Somehow, we are often hopelessly out of place in the gunmetal gray institutions of education in America. Gritty, dull, and sterile, they carry our presence like the sill carries the crane. Often, we make no sense to our surroundings, and yet we hang on, day after day, shining in our corners, miraculously surviving. Like the origami crane, a diversity of women leaders can contribute in new and surprising ways to the institutions they live and work in. They can be unexpected gifts to the world of schools, bringing color, joy, and hope to everyone who passes. They can, if they are allowed to survive. Yet it is more than being allowed. There is a stubborn persistence in the survival of that crane, something that refuses to die, despite the delicate appearance and tiny size against the massive stone building.

We need to know the secrets of that crane, how she stands so sturdy and shining, how she endures, how she manages to glow against the gritty cobwebs of her corner. It is our hope that this book reveals some of those secrets for you—ways for all of us to not only survive but to thrive in our various corners, making a difference, each in our own individual way. We can be gifts to each other, to our students, to all who pass, if we but learn to both survive and thrive in schools whose chief aim is to educate all children. This book is dedicated to all of us and to that tiny red crane, still singing in the corner of a stone bathroom stall on the second floor of an educational institution.

To the many women who have inspired us and courageously forged our paths, to the women who walk with us, and to the women who follow—
"Kulia i ka nu'u" (Reach for the summit).

1

Thriving on Variety

The Carriers of Song, Story, and Dance

*Nature thrives on variety, not monotony. Today's tall and
flawless long-stemmed roses can likewise be beautiful to
behold, but they lack the rich, heavy perfume of their less
hybridized relatives. A common topic among those
concerned with the natural world is the importance of
genetic diversity, the risk of the current emphasis on a few
high-yield species, the danger of hybridization. This
phenomenon, of being seduced by the safety of uniformity,
also confronts the Latino population and, in fact, all of us
in the country. I write, in part, to resist that myth of
safety.*

—Pat Mora (1993, p. 15)

We come to the writing of this book from different passages, yet the
journey we have made is a testament to the strength of our spirits
and the power of the stories that we tell, stories that are filled with
meaningful connections to a rich past, a dynamic present, and a future of possibility and imagination. At the same time, these stories
reveal feelings of discomfort, alienation, and fear. Fear is a very real
part of the minority experience, a haunting specter that challenges
each woman's integrity and blocks her ability to connect to others

1

and to the collective effort to build community. Perhaps the best stance is that adopted by Audre Lorde (1978a, p. 32) in her poem, "A Litany For Survival":

> and when we speak we are afraid
> our words will not be heard
> nor welcomed
> but when we are silent
> we are still afraid
> So it is better to speak
> remembering
> we were never meant to survive.

Because of (or perhaps in spite of) this fear, each of the minority women in this study has carefully offered her work to the world of education and has found, somewhere in time, a deafening silence. The stories are compelling, poignant, and loving as well as piercing, biting, and sharply insightful. They examine both the personal-private as well as the professional-public layers of these women's lives as they illuminate alternative views and voices in the world of educational bureaucracies. Each woman brings to the search for collective community and social responsibility an endeavor to "re"write her own professional life script on two levels: first, as a public expression, a story that is different from the school's prescribed, uniform pattern and second, as a personal expression, a song from within her that presents a sense of each woman's own identity that is deeply influenced by gender, race, culture, and personal history.

Unlike middle-class Anglo women, minority women in school leadership roles often lack friends in positions of power who will advocate for their needs and dreams. Indeed, research that examines, in particular, the barriers confronted by minority women in school settings is minimal, thereby fostering an implicit view that women of color are intrinsically apolitical. This silence, which each woman identifies as dangerous and forbidden terrain, denies her access to the political and further embeds the myth that somehow, color and gender are equated with inadequacy and ineffectiveness.

Although it is true that the women's movement, largely composed of Anglo women, has pressed their request to be included in the social contracts of the day, much of their work lacks the voices of minority women. The reasons for this are complex and not the thrust of this book. We would argue that the language of the women's movement, as it focuses on individual rights and access, has not fully addressed the diverse voices of minority women. Although it has been an important foundation for the work we do today, it has focused too narrowly on the individual rights and responsibilities of citizens without attending to voices of difference and issues of inequity within the women's community. To transform our conceptions of leadership and community, we must first learn from our diverse stories, which are resources that offer women and men courage, guidance, solace, and means to address the loss created by racism and sexism. Why are these stories important? One response might be that we need and deserve our stories. They ground our understanding of leadership in culture and context, elements frequently missing in mainstream literature on leadership. Another is that otherwise, we might never know, truly, the contributions of ethnic minority women, the "real woman . . . passionate and powerful, tender and volatile, brave. And, above all, fierce" (Cisneros, 1991, p. 161).

In this text, we have made an effort to capture the harmony and discords of a day, the tenor of a family, the tones of a school yard, and the yearnings of both individual and collective hearts. We have, in the process, struggled to grasp the meaning of what it is like to have one foot rooted in a rich cultural lineage of traditions grounded in ceremony and stories, matriarchy, and connectedness and the other foot moving to an unfamiliar mainstream U.S. rhythm. It is the purpose of this book to present often unheard stories of the lives and contributions of diverse women school leaders, in both formal and informal positions of leadership, in an effort to begin to explore the voices that have too long been silent. Dwelling within this often unseen terrain requires that the personal conversations of each woman be felt as much as understood intellectually.

Little has been written about women school leaders, let alone minority women leaders. As Shulamit Reinharz (1994) has stated, "Until the development of feminist scholarship, few people considered the history of women to be a history at all" (p. 37). In a similar vein, few scholars felt the views of minority women educational leaders were essential to the body of literature on school administrators. Yet, Reinharz continues, "denying people a history produces socially constructed ignorance and is a form of oppression" (p. 37). We concur with Reinharz that writing biographies about women is inherently a form of protest. Thus, we offer these stories as alternative views of what it means to be a school leader, views steeped in a rich array of cultural pasts and encompassing various ethnic and sexual orientations. These are voices from the margins, voices not often heard in mainstream U.S. culture, voices that offer the wisdom of the alternative view, voices that reframe the U.S. educational agenda through new insights and understandings about what is important and what is not in the education of America's children.

Telling the Stories
of Diverse Women

Concern about "re"defining one's own life story is pervasive in current feminist literature. Carolyn Heilbrun (1988), for example, in *Writing a Woman's Life*, critiques biographies and autobiographies of women's lives. Bell hooks's (1994a, 1994b) works advocate a dialogue engaging a progressive and holistic pedagogy among teachers and encourage a "different" story to be written about race, sexuality, and class boundaries (see *Outlaw Culture: Resisting Representations* and *Teaching to Transgress*). The narratives of other silent women are found in *I Answer With My Life: Life Histories of Women Teachers Working for Social Change* (Casey, 1993).

Yet researchers examining the knowledge and practice of school leadership have paid relatively little attention to the differences in beliefs and practices of minority women, tending instead to adopt a celebratory and inspirational stance or completely ignoring the fact that a different pattern exists. It is impossible to write the stories of minority women educational leaders without confronting oppression, encountered either by these women as children or in educational bureaucracies and society as adults. As Reinharz (1994) asserts,

> The biographer knows that the very qualities of being active and creative—if the subject of her biography has these two attributes—made the woman about who she is writing seem unusual to others, perhaps dangerous, certainly difficult to love. (p. 47)

Two essential characteristics of leaders are being active and creative, thus ensuring that to step into the role means a woman is likely to encounter conflict between what it means to be a woman and what it means to be a leader. Bloom and Munro (1995) argue,

> Our very understandings of terms like power and authority are located in and dependent on gendered understandings in which male behavior is constituted in opposition to female behavior. To be female is to not have authority. Thus, to be a female administrator is necessarily a contradiction in terms. (p. 104)

Why has there been so little attention paid to narrative accounts of school leadership presented by minority women? There can be several interrelated practical, theoretical, methodological, and political reasons. First, on a practical level, there are few minority women in traditional school leadership positions, such as school superintendents and principals, to study (see Dunlap & Schmuck, 1995; Grady & O'Connell, 1993; Ortiz, 1982; Schmuck, Charters, & Carlson, 1981; Shakeshaft, 1989). There are still fewer women, much less ethnic women, who are conducting research exploring issues of difference among their K-12 (kindergarten through 12th grade) colleagues in university departments of educational administration (Matthews, 1986).

On a theoretical level, leadership that focuses on the activities of teaching and learning by making connections between diverse children, between children and their teachers, between classrooms and families, and between schools and their neighborhoods has not been clearly identified as the "work" of school leaders. Talking about school leadership as a pedagogical issue has recently been legitimized through Sergiovanni's (1994) rich narrative in *Building Community in Schools*. His treatise suggests the need for a balance of moral leadership and skillful management in *Moral Leadership: Getting to the Heart of School Improvement* (Sergiovanni, 1992). This work and the ethical framework presented by Rost (1992) in *Leadership for the Twenty-First Century* speak to the concepts of virtue, connectedness, and mutual purpose as the work of all school leaders and against the traditional ideas of utilitarian theories, the social contract, and relativistic ethics.

In addition, the recent work of Lambert et al. (1995), in *The Constructivist Leader*, speaks eloquently to the creation of connection and community as a major concern of school leaders today. The emphasis Schon (1983, 1991) places on reflection and reflective practice in *The Reflective Practitioner: How Professionals Think in Action* (1983) and *The Reflective Turn: Case Studies In and On Educational Practice* (1991) also promotes the idea that women and men must think deeply, beyond the myths and stereotypes of "great leaders," about the work of school leadership. Last, there is a growing body of work that expresses a concern for a clear language that is inclusive of women leaders of color (see Casey, 1993; hooks, 1994a, 1994b; Sleeter, 1992; Sleeter & Grant, 1994). These passionate works have the ability to move and encourage us to further our own research and to address serious questions of "what is," "who does," and "how is" school leadership exercised.

Another difficulty of research through narrative or story, on a methodological level, is that due to its messiness, the narrative style is often regarded as merely anecdotal. In addition, narrative methodologies have focused primarily on the experiences of teachers rather than administrators (see the work of Clandinin & Connelly, 1986, 1990), although recent research has begun to examine the use of narrative in the study of school administration (see Cooper & Heck, 1995). Lieblich and Josselson (1994) believe that "we are not yet at the stage of having a theory of the narrative in the social sciences" (p. xi). Yet, like these two scholars, we "are not after a definition, but after intelligent applications of the use of narrative and its use for the understanding of human lives" (p. xi). We would argue that to talk meaningfully about *how* life experiences shape one's work as a school leader requires a storied approach that is descriptive, personal, and concrete. Stories are inescapably pervasive in our lives as they frame the foundation of our soul and have the power to shape the present and future of our lives (Kelly, 1955). It is through story that we come to know our own values, beliefs, attitudes, behaviors, relationships, rituals, and traditions. This work has been taking shape in Belenky, Clinchy, Goldberger, and Tarule's (1986) *Women's Ways of Knowing: Development of Self, Voice and Mind*, which defines *voice* as an instrument through which we gain a greater sense of self and further make meaning in the world. Stories of practitioners have been reclaimed in such works as McLaughlin and Tierney's (1993) *Naming Silenced Lives: Personal Narratives and the Process of Educational Change*, Allen's (1986) *The Sacred Hoop: Recovering the Feminine in*

American Indian Traditions, and Witherell and Noddings's (1991) *Stories Lives Tell: Narrative and Dialogue in Education.*

In addition, there is a growing body of literature that supports story as an essential component of understanding how educators think (Carter, 1992; Diamond, 1990; Jalongo, 1992; McEwan, 1992; Pagano, 1990). Perhaps the rationale for the use of stories is a personal matter. Narrative methods might very well be more responsive to the researcher's and practitioner's intent to bring to the surface those experiences that go beyond superficial masks and stereotypes. In part, it is through narrative or story that we, the authors, and the women in this book have been able to navigate our own discoveries regarding professional and personal identity as well as look to balance the paradoxes of living both on the margin and at the center.

A final reason for the relative absence of narrative studies of school leadership is political in nature. Exposing different perceptions and practices through narrative may spirit dialogues regarding issues of race, gender, class, and sexual preference that might deepen our understanding of diversity. Quite bluntly, such an understanding, grounded in a comparative examination of many different stories that address school leadership from other than an ethnocentric bias, places at risk current bureaucratic leadership practices. At this level, we might begin to move beyond the telling of stories to a deeper interrogation of the social-political institutions in which our lives are embedded.

Current discourse has been grounded in notions that have delegitimized the knowledge and life experience offered by African Americans, Asian Americans, Chicanos, Mexican Americans, Native Americans, and women (Freire, 1970, 1985; Giroux, 1992). Although some powerful stories have been written by white males (see George Noblit, 1993), Michele Foster (1992, 1993) asserts that very few first-person narratives have been written about the African American teaching experience. As we searched for stories written by ethnic minorities about their own school experiences, we found some examples in history, anthropology, sociology, and a small but growing body of stories in education (see Casey, 1993; McLaughlin & Tierney, 1993). Even fewer exist that recount the life stories of K-12 school leaders. In addition, as Foster (1993) observed, if a story was found, often, the text portrayed a heroic icon or a minority teacher or school leader who conformed to the mainstream structure and rarely fought for equity.

The Craft of Making Stories

Narrative knowledge, it has been argued (see Bruner, 1986), is more than mere emotive expression, it is a legitimate form of reasoned knowing. This type of knowing "captures in a special fashion the richness and the nuances or meaning in human affairs" (Carter, 1992, p. 6). Stories carry a multiplicity of meanings that accommodate ambiguity and dilemma as central features or themes. They help construct our personal identities and reveal life changes (Kelly, 1955), enabling us "to organize, articulate, and communicate what we believe . . . and to reveal, in narrative style, what we have become as educators" (Jalongo, 1992, p. 69). In addition, teaching narratives have been used as the basis for faculty development and evaluation (see Wood, 1992).

Just as stories have become an essential element of revealing teachers' thinking (Connelly & Clandinin, 1990), stories can frame the foundation, collect the wisdom, and shape the present and future knowledge and practice of school leadership. Cooper and Heck (1995) assert that using narrative inquiry in the study of school administration provides us with rich possibilities for understanding "how personal values, political pressures, and organizational concerns are translated into actions that are intended to solve day-to-day school problems" (p. 195). Thus, narrative as research method provides us with glimpses of previously hidden reflections on school-life phenomena rather than the traditional quantified external views provided by earlier studies. Narrative inquiry can also provide school leaders with tacit knowledge of the field as they navigate multiple realities. In the case of minority women, these multiple realities are influenced by considerations of gender and culture. Life history narratives provide us with a rich source for examining the construction of a gendered self-identity. Bloom and Munro (1995), in their study of female administrators, found these women's lives to be sites of conflict and fragmentation, rejecting the notion of a unitary self. Instead, the authors assert a "feminist, postmodernist position in which subjectivity is thought to be nonunitary—always active and in the process of reproduction" (p. 99). Given the existence of conflict and fragmentation in the lives of white female school leaders, how much more likely are we to find it in the lives of minority school leaders who are struggling with two forms of alienation, gender and race?

By attending to the ways in which these particular women leaders' life experiences affect their professional work, this text adds a rich multiplicity of layers to the understanding of administrative work. It is, for us as well as the participants, the beginning of an interesting and thoughtful journey that greatly affects how we come to know and think about ourselves, our relationships, and our professional lives.

Uses of Narrative
Theory and Construction

There are many avenues through which a researcher-biographer can approach the examination of how lived experiences and relationships with others frame ways of knowing and ways of doing. The use of narrative theory and construction has been widely employed in psychology (see Bruner, 1986; Sarbin, 1986) and in educational research (see Carter, 1992; Clandinin & Connelly 1986, 1990; Connelly & Clandinin, 1990; Elbaz, 1990, 1991). Clandinin and Connelly (1990) assert that embedded in teachers' practice resides much knowledge about the theory and practice of teaching: "Deliberately storying and restorying one's life (or, as we shall see, a group or cultural story) is, therefore, a fundamental method of personal (and social) growth . . . [and] a fundamental quality of education" (p. 259). Thus, stories have both an epistemological function, in that they contain and embody important knowledge, and a transformative function, because they leave us with altered states of consciousness, new perspectives, and changed outlooks (Jackson, 1995).

Not only do stories shape and transform our thinking, but the resulting new perspectives help shape the educational worlds we live in. As Matilda White Riley (1988) suggests,

Like the earth itself, societies endure, but not without change. As social structures change, the lives of individuals embedded within them are also altered. And, in turn, these altered lives produce further changes in society. This theme, at least as old as the Scriptures, is often taken for granted. Yet its meanings are perennially new. (p. 23)

Indeed, one's work—or art—is, as Susan Krieger (1991) writes, an expression of the self. This self is a product of social and cultural structures and norms and, in the case of the stories presented here, a self that has made many border crossings (Giroux, 1992).[1]

Narratives, then, are a valuable transformative tool. They allow us to understand the world in new ways and to help us communicate new ideas to others. This text both informs and transforms our knowledge of school leadership through the inclusion of diverse voices, those at the margins who have not been heard in the past. In most cases, Gudmunsdottir (1995) asserts, "transformation involves progressing from an incomplete story to one that is more complete and compelling" (p. 34). The stories of these women leaders in education thus provide a more complete and compelling story of educational leadership, equipping us for the multicultural school populations of the 21st century.

Simonson and Walker (1988), in *Multicultural Literacy*, state that white male academics with a Eurocentric bias, such as Hirsch, Bloom, Reagan, and Bennett, "form U.S. educational policy, and therefore our future, and they too often ignore the part that women and/or people of color play in making this culture and country what it is" (p. xiii). They assert that "other histories and cultures reveal ancestry and knowledge that has [sic] bearing on who we are and where we are going" (p. xiii). By understanding more about the lives of ethnic minority school leaders, we expand our view of educational policy and the ways in which it shapes the lives of adults and children in education today. The language of the academic world, the language of the mainstream culture, of mass media, government, business, and so on "so easily becomes abstract, distancing, manipulative. Such language cannot, with its nervous speed, its strip-mind, appropriating qualities, touch the deep, turned-over ground of our culture. Such language can, and often does, seek to bury it" (Simonson & Walker, 1988, pp. xiii-xiv). Our goal here is to unearth the stories that have been buried and to seek to use these stories to both inform and transform the world of school leadership.

Scholars have asserted that the use of stories, narratives, and personal knowledge offers an unparalleled opportunity to question many of the implicit racial, class, or gender biases that existing modes of inquiry tend to blur or mystify (see Giroux, 1992; Goodson, 1995). Thus, storying and narratology are genres that move researchers "beyond (or to the side) of the main paradigms on inquiry" and "have the potential for advancing educational research in representing the lived experience of schooling" (Goodson, 1995, p. 89). Although narrative is by no means the sole purview of women, it may be positively suited to revealing the lives of women leaders. As Lieblich and Josselson (1994) assert, "The subjective-reflective nature of the narrative coincides with the feminist ideology of compassionate, unauthoritarian understanding of the Other" (p. xii). Thus, this research joins "the work by women investigators and/or about women's lives [that] has been in the forefront of alternative research paradigms in the social sciences and the humanities" (p. xii). The importance of using narratives as data in feminist research has been discussed extensively in a number of disciplines. Comprehensive discussions can be found in *Interpreting Women's Lives*, edited by the Personal Narratives Group (1989); *Researching Women's Lives from a Feminist Perspective*, edited by Mary Maynard and June Purvis (1994); and in *Exploring Identity and Gender: The Narrative Study of Lives*, *Volume 2*, edited by Amia Lieblich and Ruthellen Josselson. A particular strength of narratives is their ability (when attentively interpreted) to "illuminate both the logic of individual courses of action and the effects of system-level constraints within which those courses evolve" (Personal Narratives Group, 1989, p. 6). In addition, life history narratives focused on women have the following advantages: they can reveal the relationships between individuals and society, they describe the ways in which women negotiate their gender status in their daily personal and professional lives, and they allow the examination of the links between the evolution of subjectivity and the development of female identity (Bloom & Munro, 1995).

Potential Pitfalls of Narrative

Yet beyond narrative's great potential to represent lived experience, in our case, the lived experience of minority school leaders, there are some potential pitfalls. Storytelling began to be used by scholars "because the current modes of cultural and political analysis were biased, white, male and middle class" (Goodson, 1995, p. 97). Goodson further asserts that although these oppositional discourses have achieved some success in representing "silenced voices," the narratives have, for the most part, remained "ensconced in the particular and the specific" (p. 97), when there is a real need for them to develop linkages to cultural and political analysis. With Goodson, we see these women leaders' stories "as a starting point for active collaboration" and a beginning of the "process of deconstructing the discursive practices through which one's subjectivity has been constituted" (Middleton, 1992, p. 20).

Although the ways to view the genre of narrative will evolve as more biographies of diverse women school leaders are collected, we have drawn from two streams of thought: postmodern and critical theory.[2] In this study, we have attempted to bridge the realms of the postmodernist and the critical theorist to understand the silenced lives of these minority women school leaders (see Tierney, 1993). In brief, we embrace the postmodern notion that life is full of rich events, critical moments (Cooper, 1994; Tripp, 1994) that involve conflicts and quiescence, differences and resemblances, the yin and yang (Rosenau, 1992). Hence, to understand the life of an individual means to uncover layers that reveal the historical, the political, the cultural, and the subconscious. To examine at a life, then, requires an analysis of the multiple, sometime opposing, edges of truth; the manifold narrative voices of the person (Tierney, 1993, pp. 119-120). Hence, from the postmodernist perspective, the dialogue of oppression and of difference, often silenced by a brutal and brittle social and political milieu, must be sensitively articulated. It is our hope that the ways in which these personal narratives are presented might travel beyond, in fact, contest, conventional myths about school leadership and thereby enliven the imagination and the soul.

Types of Narrative Inquiry

Polkinghorne (1988) has identified two types of narrative inquiry. Both share the general principles of qualitative research, such as working with data in the form of natural language and the use of noncomputational analytic procedures. One type, paradigmatic narrative inquiry, gathers stories for data and uses paradigmatic analytic procedures to produce taxonomies and categories out of the common elements across the database. The second method, narrative inquiry, gathers events and happenings as its data and uses narrative analytic procedures to produce explanatory stories. This process involves a synthesizing of the data, configuring them into a coherent whole, rather than a separation into constituent parts. White's (1975) intensive study of three lives provides an exemplar of the use of narrative analysis in qualitative research. This method "configures events into an explanation of, for example, how a successful classroom came to be, how a company came to fail in its campaign, or how an individual made a career choice" (Polkinghorne, 1988, p. 16).

We have used a narrative-type analysis in handling the data for this text, rather than a paradigmatic-type analysis. As Polkinghorne describes, we have synthesized the data from interviews, observations, journals, and other sources to develop stories that describe each woman's understanding of her own career as an administrator, both how it unfolded within her own cultural and historical context and how she understands her profession as a school leader today. Thus, we have produced what Polkinghorne (1988) describes as "knowledge of particular situations," rather than "knowledge of concepts" (p. 21). In this case, we offer the reader knowledge of the particular situations of diverse women as they go about the business of school leadership in the United States today.

Each of the stories was written by the book's authors after a series of interviews. The interviews ranged from 45 minutes to 2 hours and were arranged around open-ended questions that asked participants for biographical information, formal schooling experience information, and sharing of stories around professional experiences and beliefs. In addition, participants were asked to define school leadership and their practice of school leadership at each of the interviews; to recount critical incidents in their lives that they felt framed their knowing and practice of leadership; and to speak to issues that angered or frustrated them, such as discrimination, oppression, or segregation. The written stories were corroborated by the participants, who had the opportunity to mask identifiers, delete events that were too personal, and add information that might enhance understanding. Many participants commented that as a result of these interviews, they have grown as school leaders, becoming more confident in their thinking and actions. We offer these stories to you, the reader, in the hope that they might foster your own growth and understanding of school leadership today.

Notes

1. Giroux (1992) refers to border crossings: "Within this discourse, students engage knowledge as border crossers, as people moving in and out of borders constructed around coordinates of difference and power" (p. 136).

2. We credit much of this thinking to W. Tierney's (1993) work retelling the story of a Native Amerindian.

Part 1

The Sharing of Lives—
Let My Spirit Soar

2

Between Rivers, Dreams, and Different Worlds

Yvonne's Story—A Latina, Algonquin, Italian Woman

That is how she learned that it is true what they say, that the wolf is the wisest of all. If you listen closely, the wolf in its howling is always asking the most important question—not where is the next food, not where is the next fight, not where is the next dance?—but the most important question in order to see into and behind, to weigh the values of all that lives, wooooooooor aieeeee th' sooooooool? Where is the soul? Where is the soul? Go out in the woods, go out. If you don't go out in the woods, nothing will ever happen and your life will never begin.

—Excerpted from "The Wolf's Eyelash"
by C. P. Estes (1995, p. 465)

When I first met Yvonne, I immediately felt that I was in the company of a kindred spirit. It was a feeling that was very old, in a sense that the bonds between our souls were connected in many past lives. As we both sat back in large easy chairs, like two wolves settling comfortably in a den before a winter storm, our conversation began,

17

without much prompting, around the idea of family: how we defined family, how this affected our relationships with others, and how we believed it defined the ways we view ourselves. Yvonne explained,

> My family unit begins with me because I am really all I have when all the other stuff is taken away. This characterizes my strength, confidence, and self-reliance. That's part of the landscape and the dynamic between how people see me and how I identify myself in relation to other people. It's really just me, and I don't mean that from an isolationist point of view because I also consider networks and extended relationships to be very important.

I found Yvonne's perspective of being the center of her own life a self-affirming position of strength, which required that she take full responsibility for her history, good or bad, for her current situations in life, and for the possibilities of her future. I asked Yvonne if my understanding of her meaning of "centeredness" was accurate. She responded,

> Well, yes, but it is not an egocentric center but a knowing, insightful, and responsible center. I'm responsible for me and the lives that I touch. It is a very big responsibility and one that is hard, and has been hard, at times, for me to accept. (Deep pause.) My *nagual*, or animal spirit, is the she wolf. Because of this, I cannot deny who I am and who I am in relationship to the bigger universe.

My soul was on fire! As Yvonne spoke about her *nagual*, I thought of my *aumakua* (family guardian), the white *pueo* (owl), which has also defined my relationships and my responsibilities to others. As we talked about our animal spirits, Yvonne became animated and lucid:

> Yeah! The she wolf and the owl are strong metaphors for life. For me, the she wolf is the protector of the pack. The teacher of the pack. It is a very solitary position to be in: the alpha female. I'm canine. I mean, some people are felines, some are equines, and some are bovine. I just happen to be canine. There is no question

about my caniness. (Great laughter.) When I get around feline people, I feel real canine! Now, I'm not a coyote. I'm not quite that much of a trickster. Being a she wolf has come to me in a very spiritual way. I am the protector and teacher of my family. I am the person who keeps it together.

Capturing a Dream

In fact, Yvonne is the founder and principal of the only elementary school of choice in a large urban city. Her successful negotiation through multiple layers of an inner-city school bureaucracy is testament to her tenacity, commitment, and championship of issues focused on equality, diversity, and democracy. The school is grounded on the belief that children learn in an environment that is safe; in which everyone is welcome and belongs; where learning and teaching are meaningful and productive; and extended liaisons with parents, neighborhoods, and larger communities are valued. Teaching is multilingual, and the curriculum is multicultural and interdisciplinary, with the arts, humanities, global learning, and critical thinking woven into every learning experience.

For many years, Yvonne had a dream of opening a school that was "all about kids." Hanging in a place of prominence in Yvonne's office is a black and white painting of an African American woman teacher singing with a chorale of happy children in an urban playground framed by a brick building and a chain-link fence. The teacher wears a light chiffon dress that blows freely in a light breeze, and her engaging facial features are accented by her bold earrings and necklace. The children, all ethnic minority, are vigorously singing, clapping, and stomping their feet. Yvonne explained that she saw the picture at an art show in Sharon, Texas, "and I knew I had to have it because it said everything that needed to be said about schools. It was a picture of my dream school." Although she had very little money, she and her husband agreed to pay the $200 price tag: "It was a symbol of my dream, and I knew some day I would have a special school, and this painting would hang in my office."

Through our interviews and my visits to her school, it became apparent that this three-story, urban elementary public school of choice and Yvonne's office in the school embodied who she is as a teacher and school leader. Yvonne's cozy office is filled with cultural artifacts from South American and Central American countries. A sofa invites the tired to take respite, the many green plants and large picture window are reminiscent of a warm sunroom, and the multi-ethnic music quietly playing from the corner of her office where a teapot puffs hotly says, "Stay awhile." Besides her bookshelf, which is filled with books that explore effective leadership and good teaching, and the computer flashing its blue-streaked screen saver, there's not a clue that you're sitting in a principal's office. Yvonne says about her office,

> I want the children to know who I am. I want the children to know all the little nooks and crannies about me that will help them to interact with me more authentically. Then, we can get beyond the roles and have some good discourse. Environment is important to me. When the children, parents, or teachers come into this office, I want them to know that this isn't about power. I've got it, you don't. It's about them and me as individuals. I want them to know me and that I am open to them. The way that this school building looks and feels is just as important. I want kids to come to school to think and learn. So, this school needs to be a comfortable and safe environment for them. [She refers again to the black and white painting.] The woman in the picture is us. She's me, she's you, she's who she is. She is every woman educator. The painting solidified for me the importance of a school that is bigger than just a building. School is the relationship between all the people, actors and players within the school environment, that bring their activities and life stories to impact kids.

Yvonne continued talking about the kids in the painting. They were symbols of the many kids, ethnic minority children living in inner cities, that she has worked with and continues to be devoted to: "They are full of life and courage, but they are at crossroads in their life. They can go down one road, which is to the streets, or down another, which is to stay in school." She is often critical about the work of public schools, which she charges is restrictive, exclusive, and often ignorant of the needs of urban city children. Because of this, the elementary school's mission is symbolic of Yvonne's commitment to learning as a dynamic process that focuses on diversity, in authentic ways, and links many communities and public and private services together to benefit children. Yvonne is passionate in her criticism of school institutions' complacency about issues of diversity and multicultural education:

> For example, the purpose of all these literacy movements are focused on wanting people to learn how to read and write, but not really! Because when "they" learn how to read and write, all of a sudden "they" know what's happening to them. Well, I really think that sort of mentality exists within our public school system in a variety of areas. We are always talking about this individual blossoming, and you know, being self-reliant. Then all of a sudden, when it happens, BOOM! Some people will say, "Wait, you can't do that! You can't be too self-reliant!" Well, wait a minute, there's a mixed message here. We want children to be critical thinkers without being critical? Is this possible? Of course not! Paulo Freire talks about the curriculum, its intention, being a reflection of society. Well, I believe our curriculum says, "We don't want you to be mentally engaged in social issues because you might change the conditions, and those who are currently in power don't want to have to step down or share their power!"

On Growing Up Different

I could see Yvonne's canine ears standing erect, a bit of bristling fur standing on end down her back, and the hunter's clarity of focus in her eyes. She talked passionately about the responsibility and the promise of schooling. Yvonne began sharing her own school experiences, which she said started in the doll house of her kindergarten classroom:

> The first thing I remember about school was being in kindergarten [in a U.S. school], and being repeatedly put in the doll house. Mrs. Stebe put me in the doll house, which was in a corner of the room. I was repeatedly excluded from group activities because the group was always doing something that I already knew how to do. Like writing my name or knowing the alphabet, things like that. My mother was a teacher and my father was a school principal, so, they had worked a lot with me. I had a lot of informa-

tion and skills before I went to kindergarten. It was really sort of a punishment for knowing what other kids didn't know.

Exclusion becomes a prevailing theme in many of Yvonne's stories about her kindergarten, high school, and college experiences in the United States. This theme of being punished for being different contrasts with her liberating and self-affirming learning experiences in first through eighth grades in Brazil, Mexico, and Chile. As a child of a U.S. diplomat, Yvonne's family moved to Fortaleza, Ceará, Brazil, in 1958. Their next move, in 1962, found them in Guadalajara, Jalisco, Mexico. This was followed by a move to Santiago, Chile, in 1964. It was in this international venue that Yvonne was introduced to a world of "joyful learning and challenging, stimulating discussion." The international mix of students in attendance at the schools opened many doors to different languages and cultures. Today, Yvonne speaks Portuguese, Spanish, Italian, and English. She became an active learner, absorbing the richness of world literature and fine arts and becoming skillful in debates about global politics and governance. Yvonne says of these experiences,

> You were never treated as if you knew nothing or was supposed to know nothing. In seventh grade, we read J. D. Salinger, Neruda, Márquez, Hugo. Because kids were from everywhere, we had the most incredible and challenging education. The teachers were a powerful group of great thinkers. I mean, my geography teacher had hitchhiked down the Pan Am Highway, my biology teacher was the codiscoverer of streptomycin, and my geology teacher had been on Hillary's expedition and had spent the prior year in Chile on a major National Geographic expedition looking for Noah's ark. One of my teachers had been the coscreenwriter for the *Night of the Iguana* with Tennessee Williams. At our first class, this teacher read us *A Perfect Day for Banana Fish*. We were respected individuals!

Her teachers in Latin America were never condescending but spoke with her as if she had something important to say. In addition, the teachers took the time to get to know, in meaningful ways, the students in their classes. The impact of her school experiences in South America translates to much of her current work as a teacher, leader, and school administrator. Spending a day with Yvonne, I observed how closely she listened to children, teachers, parents, the bus driver, the janitor, the community coordinator, the curriculum specialist, and the teacher's aide. A teacher passing me in the hall stopped suddenly and without solicitation said, "She respects us and we love her. We don't want any child leaving here without feeling cared for and loved. That's what Yvonne teaches us." As a recent recipient of the coveted Milken Family Foundation award, much recognition and celebration has filled her days. In a letter to the faculty, Yvonne wrote,

> We are here because of our students. Our students are here because of their parents. Our parents are here because our district has provided them with an exciting option for their children's education. We are all connected. The acknowledgment I have just received belongs to you as well.

School: A Place
for All Families

Indeed, the work of the school is impressive. The environment is just as one would expect. The walls are covered with children's art, children's writing, and pictures of children and their families. The names that appear proudly on the artwork and poetic writing are represented in 32 national flags (Yvonne said several were at the cleaners) that circle their tiny gymnasium, which also doubles as the cafeteria. In one classroom, an old bear-clawed bathtub filled with pillows cradles a child engrossed in reading a novel (it was in Portuguese). A piano sat across the room from the reading child in a tub, its glistening black and white keys awaiting the expertise of the music teacher. In other rooms, I found soft chairs, comfortable carpeting, and children engaged in multiple projects.

In several upper-grade-level classes, I observed teachers facilitating discussions around ideas that students had generated. The teacher would challenge each student to think more deeply about these ideas and engage them actively and substantively in dialogue. Students were not hesitant to talk, even with a stranger listening in. In a fourth-grade room, the teacher had asked the children to think more critically about the masks that they had drawn, depicting a society they had been studying, and to explain how their masks told the story of that society. In another class of kindergartners, I overhead a teacher asking children for their thoughts about different themes in a book. Students poured out their ideas, and the teacher responded in positive, affirming ways. I visited the busy computer room, media center (library), and many classrooms. Everywhere I went, I was met with bustling teachers, laughing and engaged children, children listening to one another, and teachers in deep conversation with their peers and children. I asked Yvonne if all this activity was normal or was this an effect of my visit. She laughed heartily and explained that it was normal. Since the opening of the experimental school, regiments of visitors have trampled through the school: "We have had so many visitors, we're use to it. The teachers and students will always acknowledge the visitor, but they'll get on with their business."

For much of the day, I meandered from one room to another talking with students and teachers, watching and listening, and even being taught a thing or two in a variety of different languages. The whole experience was a feast, a family affair. There wasn't a sense of coldness, of exclusion or tracking, or a deep, dark current of fear, or petty jealousy and distrust. The school that Yvonne had worked so hard to create is "all about kids." There was something distinct about my experience that day in this particular school. What I felt was "love" and a deep appreciation, acknowledgment, and value for differences. When I left, Yvonne gave me two slim paper-bound booklets that were deeply moving. The first, titled, "Family Traditions: Essays from our Communities," embraces the family stories of teachers, parents, community members, and children. Each story is intimate and personally revealing. Yvonne said about the book, "We did this in celebration of our first anniversary, and it includes some of the most incredible pieces of literature. We sent a copy to the United Nations." The introductory comments read,

> Recognizing that families throughout the world are diverse in their makeup, we can appreciate the fact that the world's nations represent equally diverse and sometimes conflicting aspirations. As much as we in this country are a nation of families, the United Nations is a family of nations. Our family is also diverse and unique. We consider this fact to be an important source of strength, challenge, and inspiration. . . . The stories capture pre-

cious memories from the past, present-day traditions in-the-making and the hope that each family's traditions will thrive in a peaceful future.

The second book is titled, "Family 1994-1995 Yearbook." It's not a slick, professional school yearbook with posed student pictures but a montage of children and events, families and teachers, artwork and lasting friendships that celebrates this family of love and respect and the "multiple rings of our community." Yvonne admits that although a professionally made yearbook seemed "nice" and "cute" and parents would pay for them, it just didn't seem to mirror the activities and dynamics of the children. Candid pictures were taken of all the children in groups and in locations of their choice. With a small grant, the entire project was funded, and every family had a book at no cost. Yvonne notes,

> This is a tangible example of what is possible if everybody takes part. It is building community and responsibility. This reveals the lives and the stories of what was going on in each of the classrooms. Even the parent meeting pictures are a part of the story. Oh, here's a picture of my parents at a meeting. You know, my parents are former educators and administrators. This was a way for me to carry on the legacy, to say to them, who paved the way, here is the product of what you taught me about leadership, about networking, about possibilities, about going the extra mile.

Yvonne's maternal lineage has become a strong foundation in her life. She lovingly shared the story of her *nonna* (maternal grandmother) who came to the U.S. at the age of 27 through Ellis Island from Genoa, Italy. Pinned to her coat was a paper that read, "Eliseo De Maso, 490 East 44th, Battle Creek, Michigan." The story goes that her grandfather had left Italy, taking their newborn son, to find work in the U.S. It had been nearly 8 years before they could send for *nonna*. When she finally arrived in New York, there was no one to greet her, but her tag helped others to direct her to a train that took her to Battle Creek, Michigan. After 8 years and a very long journey over sea and land, she finally arrived at the doorstep of 490 East 44th:

As my grandmother tells the story, she knocked on the door, and my uncle John, my grandfather's brother, opened the door and said, "Maria, *bienvenatti!*" and so on and so on. He yells, "Eliseo, you know, it is Maria!" So, Eliseo, my grandfather, comes running out, gives her a big hug and says, "*Adessa cafe!*" which means, now make coffee for everyone. In other words, get to work in the kitchen. (laughter) That's the way it was.

Yvonne's *nonna* was well-educated, came from an extremely wealthy Venetian family, and was married to Eliseo for 60 years, during which time she raised six kids. The qualities of her *nonna's* character that have become pillars in Yvonne's life include hard work, commitment, introspection, and the love of cool, pastoral mountain scenes. *Nonna* taught Yvonne three important lessons:

My *nonna* left me three credos to live by. "*Cada perro tiere sudia,*" or "Every dog has its day." "*Mejor estar sola que mal acompanada,*" or "Better to be alone than poorly accompanied." And, "*No hay pan duro cuando tieres hambre,*" or, "When you are hungry, there is no such thing as hard bread." Think about it; it's all true.

Lessons Learned About School
Leadership: "El Tiempo Dira"

Often in Yvonne's talk about teaching and school leadership, she refers to the importance of making connections, thinking ahead, giving credit to others, not complaining without presenting a solution, and learning but being careful with knowledge because it can be both a destructive and creative tool. Many of the lessons she has learned by being "knocked about the real world," but she also attributes them to her mother's example. She called her mother a "Webber! I mean that woman is a spider. She just weaves everything together." As an embassy wife, she knew the importance of building relationships that extended beyond the family, the city, and the country. As a capable, educated, and articulate woman, she became an asset to Yvonne's father. Yvonne remembers also that her mother often encouraged her to get out in the world and learn. This message became clear in 1969 when Yvonne nearly lost her mother to ovarian cysts:

She almost did not make it. It was a major wake-up call for me. She had two ovarian cysts the size of grapefruits, and one of them had exploded. This put her in a coma for several weeks. My life was in upheaval because my dad isn't the strong-willed, self-disciplined person that my mother is. He went around with this angst. Anyway, my mother always said to me that it was important to get an education. That there was no other primal reason for an education than to be able to support and depend upon yourself. To be independent. I know this to be true for me, and I believe it is important to children.

Yvonne's husband and soul mate, Victor, is important to mention because he was a part of all of our conversations. That is, he was never physically present, but I heard and felt his presence whenever Yvonne spoke. Their friendship reaches far back to 1976 to the Yucatan. At the time, Victor was the captain of a ferry that transported people and goods between the island and the mainland. Because Yvonne was intrigued by Victor's quiet native pride, she shadowed him for nearly 3 days.

After about 3 days, he asked me if I was an anthropologist. He said, "If you are an anthropologist, tell me now because I don't want to go through this with me being the Mayan and you being the white woman." I said, "I'm not an anthropologist. I just think you are fascinating, and I just want to be your friend because you have this charisma, this air about you that is challenging."

They remained friends over the next 12 years even though Victor lived and worked in his home country and Yvonne returned to the United States where she married then divorced. In 1988, she returned to the Yucatan to see how Victor was doing. As Yvonne explained, "Victor said, 'Well, do you want to do it [marriage] now, or do you want to wait until we're 70?' I said, I think now would be a real good time." Their union has nurtured Yvonne's sense of direction and leadership. For example, Victor, a full-blood Mayan, is proud of his ancestry and resents activities that serve to assimilate him to values that are not innately part of his history. This clarity provides him with direction and defines how he relates to people, how he makes decisions, and how he sees the world. Yvonne's breath is sweet as she talks about Victor:

He is Mayan. There is no Spanish surname anywhere in his lineage. He is very proud of that. He is very much in touch with time, the time that Mayan people and indigenous people have been around. He is rooted in tradition from a completely spiritual standpoint.

Yvonne has taken many of Victor's thoughts to heart. For example, Victor's sense of time is translated in his saying, *"el tiempo dira,"* time will tell me when I'm going to do this. The concept of letting time help one make a decision is a dimension of thinking that Yvonne applies to her vision and to her work. This, of course, flies in the face of current administrative activity that requires quick decisions made by a sole authority. To think of time as a tool and not an enemy requires a very different way of thinking about one's position and work as a school leader. Although putting out fires seems to come with the landscape, Yvonne knows that because she is in the business of teaching children, decisions need to be made thoughtfully and with great care. How does Yvonne resolve this very real tension of displaced time? She explains,

> Well, we all live between two worlds. I've lived between two worlds all my life. Because of this, I've had to learn to negotiate those two different parts of my life. Time is a major negotiating point with teachers and others. You must wonder why and how an individual sees certain priorities differently than you. For example, for the last 5 to 6 years, I've had to deal with a lot of political stuff to get this school of choice to happen. Had I been more anxious about time, I probably wouldn't have realized this venture. I wouldn't have thought it out, and I probably would have politically beat up on people. Instead, I have many allies. Time as a negotiating tool also defines relationships, and it is an extremely collectivist perspective. We're doing this together, and we're thinking about this together.

Another theme from Victor's life that has deeply affected Yvonne's values and ways of working is his understanding of survival. Because Victor was financially unable to attend a formal school, his feelings of exclusion and desperation led him to build his own learning structures that enabled him to be resourceful and self-reliant. This story is not Yvonne's, but she admits it is the story of many students and their families who populate urban schools. It is also a story that many school leaders neglect because they get caught up negotiating the "other stuff of school administration, not the important stuff that focuses on kids."

Yvonne is very clear that the work of schooling is not the work of an individual but of a collective body that is linked in often unique and sometimes complicated ways:

> I don't see myself as being central to other individuals' lives. I mean, I might be a piece, but I'm not central. I still don't think I'm central to the creation of this school, but I understand my impact on it. I understand my responsibility to it and with it. It is a very collaborative mutual vision and effort. It is dynamic and not static. I know that's a very different way to look at it. It's the Anglo world view that you can freeze-frame life. That if you just get all of the actors and props and scenario together, you can take a picture of it and say, "Look! This is what schools look like." Or "Look! This is what leadership looks like."

It was at this point of our conversation that I became curious about Yvonne's sense of leadership. I began to search Yvonne's words, cutting between her shadow and her physical figure, listening for what it means to be a champion of ideas and a participant of engaging learning experiences. The answer was illustrated in her husband's skilled Mayan artistry and in a wooden lapel pin that Yvonne had carved of a woman carrying a baby. In reviewing my many notes and transcripts, I began to realize that Yvonne is an artist in the truest sense of the word. For myself, art is a means of connecting the soul to the seasons of one's journey. That is, art reveals where a person has been and, like stepping stones across a swift stream, marks a path for others to follow. Yvonne's artistry is revealed in her appreciation of Victor's work, in her own wood carvings, and in the tapestry of a rich and genuine learning environment. Her commitment to her craft is honest, passionate, insightful, and courageous because her love for children is pure. In response to my characterization of her as an artisan, Yvonne replied,

> I really am an artist, but I believe all effective leaders are artists because art is a way of looking at something. A good artist can look at something from many angles and see its possibilities. It's

like looking at an item, then breaking the paradigm completely. Totally taking that item out of its common function and putting it into a completely different form. An effective leader sees this potential. Art is also the ability to manifest something. To me, it is how we channel the potential and web it together to make something. It's the manifestation of our visions. Unfortunately, I think women, especially minority women, have the capacity to understand this potential "out there." We don't see it in ourselves.

We began to howl! Yvonne and I began to howl! If there was only one thing Yvonne and I had in common, it would be the belief that women in education cannot remain hidden or silent. What has happened, however, is that ethnic-minority women have not been included (much less invited) in the dialogue around learning and the business of schooling. This distancing from a discourse that can truly make a difference for children and youth has proved to be a formidable barrier and has taught many women that "silence pays off." If we, minority women, should howl, we are often labeled "reactionary," "troublemakers," or "that crazed so-and-so woman." Yvonne shared many examples of being told that her ideas of schooling, which she admits are truly "democratic notions of schooling, god forbid!" have often been overlooked or condemned outright.

There were many stories that we shared that spoke to what we began to name as "institutionalized dissing." Although we agreed that being silent is still being rewarded, we were optimistic that there is growing institutional support for voices with different takes on schooling to speak out. Many of the women and men who have been the catalysts for this movement have had to push through the barriers of race and ethnicity, gender, social class, language, and ways of thinking about life and equality. We have individually come to know many of these heroes who have built and continue to build new bridges in education that create space for other ethnic minority women to be "bold!" I would say that Yvonne is one such hero.

Currently, Yvonne's work is a deliberate and conscious effort to understand current power structures. She champions efforts that press the schools to address hard issues of equity, inclusion, nonelitism, and people's rights. As the president of the State Bilingual Education Association and chair of the school district's committees that focus on global and multicultural education, Yvonne has had to

draw from her experience and knowledge to play ball in the politi-
cians' sandlot. She has the courage to say what others will not say,
especially in her efforts to focus the discussion on the responsibility
to create policy that supports good teaching and is inclusive of all
members of the school, neighborhood, and city community. Yvonne
maintains her quest, fortifying new bridges that she says, "someday,
the ethnocentric, the naive, will have to cross—and then they will
know the truth."

Yvonne remarked at our last meeting,

> I think probably the most important thing is to understand the
> essence, the essence of what we're here to do. Not the details.
> Not the micro management. Not the whos, the whats, the whens,
> the wheres, the what times, the what dates. Why are we here?
> Look at the kids.

We began our discussion in the parlor of my office, two wolves
feasting on each other's energy, attending to the stories of our lives
and roving between the many worlds that we have been a part of.
We concluded our conversation 4 months later in the parlor of
Yvonne's office, two wolves still puzzling over the harmonies of life,
still writing the poetry of our lives, still circling the politics of the
school. As I left Yvonne, I truly felt that something blessed had silently and lovingly brushed me.

3

A Tale of Balance and Wit

Margaret's Story—
A Tamil Indian Woman

This ancient word yoga is pressed by the Gita into service to mean the entire gamut of human endeavor to storm the gates of heaven. . . . [It means] the yoking of all the powers of the body and the mind and soul to God; it means the discipline of the intellect, the mind, the emotions, the will, which such a yoking presupposes; it means a poise of the soul which enables one to look at life in all its aspects and evenly.

—Mahadev Desai (Gandhi's friend and secretary, as quoted in Easwaran, 1985, p. 32)

When I think of India, I see beautiful brown women dressed in saris of multiple colors, adorned with heavenly scented flowers, and lounging beside a river near a lush forest. The stories that Margaret told about her childhood and her professional experiences in India added a spiritual richness to my own images. She spoke eloquently about the jasmine flower that reminded her of her hometown in the southern part of India. Growing up in Nazareth, a Christian enclave in a predominantly Hindu society, was a unique experience.[1]

Getting to know Margaret was coming to understand her sense of balance between such opposites as Indian culture and U.S. culture,

Hindu and Christianity, caste system and equity, duty and desire, and the English language and Tamil. That her heart and intellect were large enough to embrace the complexities and contrasts in her life journeys was in itself an enlightening message. Her moral and aesthetic guides that have created her bicultural identity are deeply embedded in a philosophy and cultural context that is peculiarly both Indian and Christian. An example of this is her belief that her time on earth is only a small piece of a much larger and dynamic terrain, but it is from this current place that one can view the possibilities of the future. Margaret explained that this future orientation is deeply Hindu, as the philosophy of time and life suggest that the past and present define future life placement. Yet, this is Christian as well, for to do well in this life helps a person to enter heaven. This future orientation, pervasive throughout her story, fires Margaret's deep personal commitment to locate positive balance in her life so that she might fulfill her "duty" to family and community, that she might "achieve" in this life her fullest potential, and that the wisdom of Christ and Krishna "to be socially concerned and responsible" are primary components of her life works.[2]

Intrigued by the possible conflicts between Hindu and Christian beliefs, I listened carefully to the undersong of Margaret's life stories. Thinking that I might become privy to her personal dilemmas regarding patriarchies, caste systems, and colonialism, I envisioned listening to torrid, angry tales of marginalization and oppression. Although there were many stories about the inequity of the caste system, Margaret's vocal tone and cadence, coupled with her choice of words and her warm disposition, told stories of possibilities, stories that sought balance and stressed optimism and faith, and stories that transformed pain to compassion. She believes that because life is an opportunity to discover and to realize God while on earth, pessimism and desire could not be a part of her physical, mental, and verbal language.

Learning From Our Mothers

In addition, the belief in "duty to serve" has defined who she is, what she chooses to do, and how she goes about her work. Of significant importance is the story of her mother, who exemplified spiritual duty.

My mother's death, which wasn't expected, helped me to reflect.
I thought more about my mother's characteristics and remember
my mother as being a very giving and people-oriented person. I
want to emulate that. She was always a happy person and
wanted to be with people. She was responsible and caring and
took care of our family. When I gave birth to my own children, I
was reminded of my mother's example. I had a duty to my children and family. I know that my mother's example has influenced my own feelings about teaching because I feel a great
sense of responsibility, love, and duty to all children. Duty is a
basic concept of life in India. Your duty to your children, to your
husband, and to your family. Duty comes before anything else.
If you do all your duties, then you'll have a better birth in your
next incarnation. Although I don't believe in reincarnation, the
feeling of duty and service I have are influenced by my Christian
faith and Hindu culture.

When I questioned Margaret about this concept of duty, she
found it difficult to explain in the English language, saying, "English
isn't a very mystical language, so, it's not easy to explain these
[ideas] clearly." So what I found myself attempting to do was listen
carefully to the examples she gave of how she fulfilled her duty. It
was from these examples regarding her teaching experiences in India
and the United States that I was able to define duty as a dual strand
of living that turns inward to embrace individual struggle for self-
mastery and, at the same time, turns outward to embrace compassion toward all living creatures. It is this dialogue between an inward
and outward duty and the translation of that idea to practice that
gets to the soul of life's meaning and transcends the effects of marginalization and negative stereotypes. It is also the core that defines
Margaret's professional work and commitment to children and
youth.

Teaching in India

Margaret's first professional experience was in a college lab high
school, teaching Indian Civics and Government.

My first teaching experience in India was everything that I had dreamed about. After graduating from college with a teaching degree in secondary education and history content, I taught high school at the college's lab school. Most of the kids were very intelligent. They were the professors' children and came from rich homes. It was very challenging to teach these kids, and I enjoyed it. They wanted a lot of information. They worked me hard! I taught history, Indian Civics, and Indian Government. Oh, how I used to enjoy that. It was a very interesting experience. So, as a teacher, I was concentrating on how to get these kids to think more critically. I was challenged to think, too, because some of those kids were much smarter than me. In India, the inspectors from the State Department come to inspect the classrooms. They sit through the class, observe what's going on, and then report to the principal. During my first year of teaching 7th grade, the inspector came into my room and watched me. He wrote me up as the best teacher in the school. Because in traditional Indian instructional technique, a teacher taught straight from the textbook. But I had objects to illustrate, such as examples, calendars, maps, and stories. Besides, the students were all talking and involved in the learning process.

I was curious to know if Margaret's teaching experience had been enhanced by having such extraordinary students in her class. She admitted that it was very challenging but that she later taught seventh and eighth grade in another school with a variety of children from different social and economic backgrounds. This teaching experience, Margaret smiled, "was the real thing." She enjoyed teaching this diverse group of children who all "came to school to learn." When I inquired if this cultural attitude toward learning is pervasive, she replied that in her own experience, students felt it was

their duty to respect teachers and to work hard in school. You see, in India, the kids are there to learn—learning is a big part of our culture. I didn't have to deal with behavioral problems. There wasn't a problem of motivation because we all knew that we have to do well in school if we wanted to have a good life. This was very different from my experiences here [in the United States].[3]

One day, I was walking through the student center at the college my husband and I were attending, and someone said that a school district was looking for special education teachers. They were recruiting. So I went to sign up, never thinking that I would get a job. They wanted to interview me right away. After the interview, they offered me the job. That's how I got to this school district.

I will always remember my first year of teaching in the U.S. It was very difficult because I was new to the context. All my life, I had met Americans who were visiting India or were missionaries, but living here and having to work in this different social context was very difficult. Here I was, putting all my knowledge into teaching. I remember spending hours and hours preparing, trying to design the class and get it going. I could not succeed and had many problems managing the students. There was a different way of doing business in the classrooms. The processes of teaching and learning [were] so different. In India, I was trained to teach kids who were motivated. Motivation was not an issue. The training focused on instructional methodology: how to teach the content in the most meaningful way. So the teacher's responsibility is to add excitement to the learning, not to concentrate on motivation.

In India, I had 50-52 kids in my class and had no problems. Here I had only 10-12 kids, but I could not relate culturally and didn't know how to handle them. There was such a big gap in our cultures. Kids didn't even respect you. In India, you walk into a classroom of kids who are there waiting for a teacher. Here, the teacher is waiting for the kids. Completely opposite situations. I finally told the principal that I really needed to go and observe other classrooms. So he was very kind and gave me a visitation day. I went into another middle school. It really helped me. I also went to whatever staff development opportunity was available. I started organizing differently and learned to adapt my old methods in new ways. I had been making everything I did such a complex task. For example, my style was interactive. I would go around the class and talk with the students who were always motivated to interact with me and others. I had to change that completely here. I moved to more group-oriented projects, more hands-on activities and experiential things. Before, I was working hard to meet every one of the kids' needs without many resources. The more veteran teachers I observed and talked with had already been dealing with these barriers and had found ways to work with them. My second year of teaching was much better as I was working with a new attitude. I was transferred to another school where I found a friend and colleague. We were able to share ideas, and I'd get a lot of practical advice from her.

Feeling Like a Frog in a Well

Margaret experienced culture shock on a variety of levels. First, she recognized that she was now working with very different children, from diverse backgrounds, religious beliefs, and experiences in schooling. Margaret's comments reflected her amazement that teachers were isolated from one another, often by choice, and that many held combative attitudes toward other teachers and the school administrators. She was also struck by the lack of communication not only among the faculty and administrators but with parents and the community. Last, she had often found that her continuous inquiry, although normal in India, was not appreciated in the United States.

> So that I could function in this new system, I had to go through a learning phase. I had to be a learner. My Indian culture helped me to look at the whole system as one entity, and I sought intuitive understanding of people and their different ways of doing. What I mean is that you don't stop at the cognitive level of understanding but go to the soul. I'm always asking questions and asking for colleagues to add their ideas to any decisions that need to be made. This might be a barrier to me being promoted. The current district structure rewards a form of leadership that deals with day-to-day management, not visionary leadership. Current governance of the schools sees the administrator as the main decision maker and not a facilitator of teams who share in decision making. I disagree with that because leadership is more future looking and more community centered.

Fascinated by Margaret's assessment that she would not move any higher in the school district's governing structure, I asked her to talk more about her administrative experiences. She shared how she worked with teachers to be more reflective about their teaching through small group dialogue and journal writing: "I believe that individual understanding is important to how one adapts effective practices. I teach that teamwork has to come from the heart, otherwise it is very superficial." Margaret went on to describe her work dismantling attitudinal rifts between administration and teachers: "I work hard to nurture the staff and faculty. It is important that I respect teachers and share decision making, reward innovation, reflection, and risk taking."

> I'm not like other central office staff that talk about it and don't practice it. For example, I was the director of summer school for 3 years, for about 400 migrant children and 21 teachers. We had the teachers working in teams that met two times a week to develop curriculum and teaching strategies. We integrated science, social studies, and language arts. The teachers were very motivated and wanted to be there. We used bilingual and ESL [English as a second language] methods to teach. I worked with the teachers, and I shared decision making. I rewarded innovation, reflection, and risk taking with notes and flowers. I also told them that they were valuable to the students, the students' families, and to the community.

Margaret continues to work at the forefront of team building, believing that "authentic collaboration is powerful. . . . Teachers have the power to make change, but they need to be reflective practitioners and work together." Collaboration also includes the work of linking schools with the community. She explains that helping schools to become real learning communities had become her mission, as it seemed a natural translation of her own philosophical beliefs in self-mastery and compassion. I sensed, throughout her telling, that she had a strong desire to be promoted within her school district but had tempered this effort. Her silence about this puzzled me because it directly conflicted with a lifetime of personal and professional achievements. I thought perhaps I could understand her motives by listening more closely. Margaret told many stories of how she had navigated through the patriarchal social structure of India:

Growing up in India, you know that only in a functional sense is it a male-dominant society. It is not male-dominated in a philosophical sense because there are a lot of women gods in India. And the woman—the mother—is very important. India is called "Bharata Mada," meaning "Mother India." There is a matriarchal philosophy. In our philosophy and in our poetry, we are told that India comes first and then your mother. Your mother is the god you are able to see. India has had queens, some of them are remembered today, but historically, we only talk about kings.

The barrier, in India, Margaret most often faced was that of skin color:

The color of your skin is the center of identity. I have to tell you this because in India, color is a big issue. This brings me back to my personal life. In my home, I am the darkest. The caste system first originated on color because the Aryans (the Brahmans are the Aryans) who came to India from central Asia were fairer in skin color. The natives, Dravidians, were darker people. The Aryans didn't want to integrate with the Dravidians, the original Indians. So to maintain the division, they began the caste system. If you're of the darker shade, you have disadvantages growing up. My family didn't want me to feel or think that I was good for nothing because no one would want to marry a girl who's dark. Dark women have to give lots more dowry to get married than light women. So a darker complexion girl might be a burden to her father. I never grew up around people who said negative things about me, but I was aware of the comments. My mother was always loving toward me. In my school days, I wasn't the top student but people always said, "Yes, Margaret you can do it."

After Margaret shared her stories about the issue of skin color and how it became a motivating factor in her life, she wrote in her journal,

Whenever another Indian comments on my complexion, I wish I was fairer than what I am, but not white. However, I don't sit

and think or worry about it. I have suffered several times, especially when I was young, when adults have commented on my
skin color. Kids have never mentioned it. I've also suffered when
I'm with Indians from the North who think they are superior
because they are fairer than the Southern Indians.[4]

Margaret's stories about her sixth grade to senior high school
experience persuaded me of her dazzling educational accomplishments. Her narratives were filled with ambitions and successes that
were not easily earned. She did not have the comfort, support, and
positive environment of home during her middle and senior high
school years because, at the age of 11, she had been sent 300 miles
away to attend a Christian boarding academy. She said of this experience, "I grew up in a boarding academy. I was only 11 years old,
and I went home only for vacations." It was at this boarding school
that Margaret remembers learning the U.S. concept of *work ethic*. This
was a Protestant-Christian boarding academy with an American
principal.

> We woke up about 5:30 a.m. Then we worked on the campus
> doing various types of work. Two and a half hours of manual
> labor. We worked in the fields or cleaned the streets. That was in
> the morning. Then we had showers, breakfast, and went to
> school. Then we had worship and a study hall. The whole day
> was regimented like a military routine.

Although Margaret talked casually about this regimental rou-
tine, she took to heart the message of hard work, as it fit her belief
that it was only through her labors that she could ensure her own
success. Chance or fate were not a part of Margaret's life concept.
Beyond the 5:30 wake-up call, Margaret believes that her boarding
experience was not only academically enriching but that she learned
a valuable lesson about differences.

> I remember when I went from my home state to another state, I
> became conscious of differences in people. I saw people from
> other states in India with different food habits and clothing. Al-
> though some of our cultural habits were the same, our language
> was different. It was in this multilingual context, that I, just 12
> years old, was beginning to define my self-identity. I remember

thinking, "How could these people speak in any other language than mine?" I remember that feeling so distinctly today. So I worked hard to learn to speak in English, and I also started to understand that the world is made up of many differences.

Margaret continued this stream of thought later in her journal: "I felt like a frog in a well. I now saw a world different from mine. I had a desire to fit in with those that spoke English." When she moved to the United States, Margaret found herself teaching both adults and children about the diversity that makes up India.

Because I'm from India, people look at me very differently than the way they might look at other minorities. They say, "Oh, you're from India." They treat me with respect and ask me all kinds of questions about India, the caste system, and Gandhi. They ask me why I don't have a dot on my forehead. That's part of the Hindu culture that the Westerner has seen. They ask me about the sari and about Indian food. There has been so much romanticizing of India, it is really terribly funny the ideas some Americans have about Indian people. Other ethnic minorities ask me about my high self-esteem and cultural pride. They ask, "How did you get it?" I say that the confidence is in me. I grew up knowing I could be successful. I have never been very knowledgeable about my own cultural traditions, but more and more, I've learned to appreciate Indian dance, Indian music, and I love to watch Indian movies. I am constantly working on having a balance in my thinking. My culture is a real foundation and can sometimes be in conflict with the American culture. The way I think about balancing is to ask myself, "How can I contribute, in my unique way, to make things better here?" I bring my multicultural perspective and my belief in peaceful relations to bear on whatever I do. I work this way because I think it's important regardless of what other people may say or think.

After reading again and again her stories about recognizing differences and working toward equity, I questioned the effect the caste system might have had on Margaret. She explained,

Only our caste lived in our little town. The other people from other castes who lived outside our town were all laborers and

would serve the landowners. There was one caste that worked
in our fields; we call them Pallans. Then, there were the Barbers
who cut hair for male members in the family and took care of our
family graveyards. There were washermen, we called them Dob-
bies, the ones that wash and iron your clothes. We didn't have a
lot of association or contact with these laboring groups. I grew
up with this aloofness toward lower-caste people. It wasn't until
I went to college that I tried to break the hold of the caste system.

At the university, Margaret learned more about issues of inequity
that plagued her country and about the struggle of her own caste in
India. Margaret believes that this awakening defined her purpose
and at that moment, she transcended, in a more spiritual way, closer
to God.

I learned about the importance of unity. Unity is very spiritual
because it means living together in spite of the differences in the
setting. You know, the caste system was so divisive, but the philosophy of unity still has a cultural expectation. I was not aware
of caste rebellions when I was growing up. But when I went to
college, I learned about intercaste wars.
I believe in the idea of treating all Indians with respect and
dignity.

Margaret's commitment to break the barriers between the castes is
clearly evident in her work as a school leader in India:

I was educating the children of India to be knowledgeable about
others because there is a lot of intolerance, prejudice, and injustice against people. Teaching tolerance was my big goal because
of India's multiethnic, multireligion, multilingual population
and caste-oriented system. In my classes, I did a lot of simula-
tions such as a Hindu meeting a Moslem. Because the people
were used to segregation, I taught the children that each one of
them had value. Whenever we had a school program, I always
included a short play related to tolerance and understanding.
Whenever I see anything that relates to segregation in society,
I get very angry. I have a strong reaction to it. For example, I
remember it was the custom in our town that a lower caste
should not come into our, the Sudhra, houses. I would get very

annoyed and allow them into our house and ask them to sit in our chairs. Today, I teach about social issues, like segregation. I have students look closely at problems from a historical context and to think also of possible solutions.

Using Wit in Leadership

As I listened to the silence of Margaret's stories, I came to understand the message of her careful assessment that she might always be overlooked when it came time for leadership advancement in the district school administration. Margaret's work is grounded in a selfless act of duty that transcends boundaries created by desire. She feels strongly that her excellent works and achievements are testament to her actions and that her spiritual development has been blessed. This strong sense of self has defined her school work as transformational. That is, Margaret's work is grounded in her belief that the child-student is the center around which school professionals in partnership with parents and community work collectively to empower. Because of her beliefs, Margaret has publicly chastised political power games because, "it is a terribly destructive net of karma." She instead has chosen to network with peers, to press for ongoing conversation with teachers and parents, and to develop her own scholarship.

After reading her stories about facing adversity and recognizing differences, I came to realize she had a strong social concern for equity. This advocacy for equity did not strike Margaret as important early in her life but began at the university where she learned more about the struggle of her own caste in India. This awakening is a significant event in Margaret's life as she believes that it was at this moment she felt "an individual liberty." She explained,

> I learned about the importance of unity. Unity is very spiritual because it means living together in spite of the differences in the setting. You know the caste system was so divisive, but the philosophy of unity still was a cultural expectation.

I was curious to know how she manages to work within a school context that in many ways is unsupportive of her personal and professional beliefs. Margaret's explanation revealed that she would always be her own storyteller because a "good teacher, a good school leader is always learning and always serving children." At the end of a conversation, Margaret revealed that she would always be her own gardener:

> I remember sitting on the front porch and grandpa telling me stories. They were Indian myths. The stories talked about honesty, respect, and wit! You use your wit to get out of hard situations. I use my wits.

Notes

1. Margaret provided some historical information regarding her hometown and her ancestors that might be of interest to the reader:

> My ancestors, my great-grandfather was a Hindu as well as my great-great-grandfather on my father's side. My great-grandfather was the one who initiated the Christian movement in my town. India had been colonized by the English and became a British colony. The southern part of India was very much influenced by Christian missionaries, even before the English came. In 56 AD, according to legend, Apostle Thomas came to South India. So Christian influence started before the English and other European countries colonized India. After the Europeans colonized India, Christianity, especially in the southern part of India, became very dominant.

2. I interviewed Margaret over an 8-month period and have worked with her on a variety of school-community-related projects and graduate course work over the past 3 years. Margaret is currently a PhD candidate in education and, at the time of our interviews, held a full-time job as a team developer and professional staff developer in her district's central office. Due to the reorganization of the school district, her position was eliminated, but this is yet another story.

3. Margaret and her husband moved to the United States to continue their education. She said of this move,

> We were studying at Andrews in St. Joseph's, Michigan, which is near Notre Dame. The reason we came to America to study is because Andrews is a private Christian college recognized by the American University and Colleges. We could not go further

in our studies in India. I came to earn a master's [degree] in education, and I went into special education. Back then, in India, we didn't have special education. We only had schools for the blind, for the deaf and dumb.

4. Regarding journals: Each participant was asked to share personal and professional artifacts as well as journal reflections. In addition, each participant was asked to comment on the interview process, to use the journal as a means to supplement our interview conversations, and to write reactions to my (the author's) interpretations and writing of their stories. Some of the material used in the final stories came from these sources, but generally, much of the information was generated from the interviews.

4

A Passionate
Web of Living

Catherine's Story—
A Cuban Woman

> The engaged voice must never be fixed and
> absolute but always changing, always evolving in
> dialogue with a world beyond itself.
>
> —bell hooks (1994b)

Within the enigmatic complexities of a school webbing, Catherine weaves and reweaves her own patterned webbing. She labors daily to repair threads that have been damaged by the pull and tug of a system that is often not aligned with her own commitments as a school leader. Listening to Catherine's stories, three tensions that strain and threaten to lacerate her fragile web illuminate the differences between what it means for her to be a woman of Cuban American heritage in a school leadership position and what schooling and school leadership mean to the school institution. The issues around which she and the district leadership collide include equity, community dialogue and action, and leadership philosophy.[1]

Moving Children Out of the Boxes

Catherine is a petite Cuban woman with striking features and a rippling laugh that has a Cheshire-cat-grin feel to it. I felt a deep sense of kinship with her as many of our growing-up and coming-of-age stories were similar. At times, I felt that Catherine chose me to tell her story because, like her, I often speak out against "one-size fits all policies" and advocate against narrow and myopic educational practices. In fact, much of Catherine's telling is filled with her own work as an advocate for equity. Regarding the importance of giving every child the opportunity to learn, she recalled a significant moment in her bilingual teaching career that convinced her that she must always act on her commitment to root out stereotypes that box children in. Catherine speaks passionately about how she sees her work as a school leader.

> I am an advocate for minority children. In my last job as a bilingual teacher, I witnessed monolingual kids being tested in English. I thought, "This can't be. Not in the 1980s." The principal asked me, "Would you translate for this child?" I said, "What do you mean, translate? He needs to take the test in Spanish with a Spanish-speaking psychologist giving it to him." I talked with the psychologist, who was African American; he said, "There's nothing wrong with not giving the child the test in his own language." The reason why it was allowed to happen is because the parents never said anything. The school wanted to categorize this child as retarded! I knew he was not retarded. I took the parents aside, and I said, "Your child is not retarded. Please!" The parents would not sign the IEPC [individual educational plan contract].

Because of this and many other similar experiences, Catherine has recognized the importance of educating the families of minority children who have been ignored by an uncaring school system. Throughout her professional career, Catherine has focused on redefining the work of schools by revising the school's curriculum and instruction to address the needs of children whose primary language is not English. She explained that this has become an important priority for her, not only because it is an obvious need, but because of her own life experiences. As a young 5-year-old immigrant from Cuba, she had no advocates. Arriving in the United States in the early 1960s, she spoke Spanish and very little English:

> I remember my kindergarten class! My kindergarten teacher was an old lady, well, what I thought was really old. I remember her doing sign language to me. I had no idea what was going on. In Cuba, we used colored pencils, so when I saw crayons, I didn't know what they were. What did I do? I started building things because I thought they were Lincoln logs. I stayed in that kindergarten class, but I didn't know what was going on. I felt kind of stupid for the first three grades.

This critical event in her young life, which has caused her pain, embarrassment, and anger, impressed on Catherine the importance of placing the "child, not the teacher, not the administration" at the center of the learning experience. As a young novice teacher fluent in English and Spanish, she chose to teach in bilingual classrooms, beginning with "what the kids brought to class. . . . And I began to learn that I could correct the wrong that I grew up with."

> I did class bilingually. I explained things in Spanish and English. And I did have reading groups. One group I taught in Spanish because they were monolinguals and they didn't know any English. The philosophy was that you begin to teach them reading in their own language, and at the same time, you teach them English as a second language. I taught third grade for 9 years.

On Being a Cuban American School Principal

Catherine brings to her school principalship a successful 12-year teaching career in the states of New Jersey, Texas, and Michigan and administrative experience as coordinator of a parenting education program for a mental health agency. Although her record and references are exemplary, she commented that her professionalism and leadership ability as an elementary school principal are often questioned by her supervisors. She explained that because of her advo-

cacy for children of minority backgrounds and because she speaks
out against the school district's limited leadership opportunities for
people of color, she is often dismissed as an "angry Hispanic
woman" and not a credible school leader. As Catherine spoke these
words, her voice began to tremble and I turned off the tape recorder.
There was a long moment of painful silence as we both recalled the
shunning that had become tombstones along the river that we both
have traveled. Yet Catherine perseveres to redefine the way schools
do business.

> I don't think the district is doing enough to recruit minorities.
> Even though they say they are. I believe the district has to com-
> mit financially, put the money into education and recruitment, if
> they want to make a commitment to plurality. There's a double
> standard here and probably in other small urban centers. Even
> though there are many ethnic minorities, we still live in a segre-
> gated society. Looking within our school district, there are only
> three Hispanic principals and one assistant principal. There's
> not a whole lot of Hispanic teachers in the classrooms, either. In
> the leadership training program, there's not a lot of Hispanics. I
> think there's a difference in the way the organization "mouths"
> the way it should be and the way "it is." It's a good-'ole-boy
> system, it's a white system. Women are not valued in this orga-
> nization, let alone minority women who are assertive. There are
> principals of color who are dynamic. Women who have progres-
> sive ideas, women who are caring, women who are competent,
> but they are not in leadership positions. Now, look at our central
> office. You can count people of color in decision- making posi-
> tions on one hand! Of those people of color, some are advocates
> for equity, but most are token Hispanics and appear to be fence-
> sitters, never standing up for anything. I guess I get in trouble
> because I'm not a fence-sitter.

Catherine is anything but a fence-sitter, often acting with
courage and integrity. An example of this is her proactive work to
break down the walls between the elementary school and its neighborhood. The school enrollment is one of the largest in the district
and is composed of Hispanic-Latino, African American, and Caucasian children. This populace is considered at-risk because of its
low socioeconomic status. Because of the issues of gang violence,

drugs, prostitution, poverty, and abuse, Catherine initiated a collective community task force, which includes parent groups, neighborhood programs and associations, social and public services, churches, recreation programs, local businesses, and health facilities.

> We have an enrollment of 521, which is one of the highest. The reason we're one of the highest is because we've added an addition to our building. Last year, we had 377 students, K-5 [kindergarten through 5th grade], and did not have 6th grade. Our 6th graders had to go to the school down the street. Now, we are K-6 [kindergarten through 6th grade]. One classroom, in the 6th grade, is a special education inclusion classroom. We also have an E. I. [educationally impaired] classroom that's second- and third-grade level. The ethnic makeup includes Hispanics, African Americans, and Caucasians. The Hispanics are the highest percentage, I'd say about 75% to 80%. There's a mixture of Hispanic students that come to us, but for most, their first language is Spanish; they have no English. They come from Mexico or the Dominican Republic. We have a bilingual education program that is a pull-out program where they get the services that they need. The second highest population is African American, and Caucasian is the smaller of the three.
>
> Our population is considered at-risk because it's a very low socioeconomic population. The neighborhood is gang infested with a lot of drugs and prostitution. This is the worst area in the city because Division Street is known for its drug dealing and prostitution. We're two blocks from Division Street. Some of our students come from homes where crack is being sold. Some come from homes where their mothers are prostitutes. Not all of them, but that's the reality of some of the children who come here. We don't have the hard documented evidence that we have "crack babies" here, but we know, by observing the way some students behave in class, that there's definitely a lot of them, especially in the second-grade classes.

Admittedly, she has placed herself in the center of turbulent waters. "You see, I just didn't talk about it. I did something!" During her 4-year tenure, Catherine has worked with this strong community-school coalition to provide children and their families with a full-service, comprehensive school. There is now a neighborhood police officer stationed at the school, afterschool and summer sports and recreation activities, academic programs for all ages (K-12), early childhood care and parenting classes, adult community education classes, medical services offered at the school once a week, and an office space that is used by a variety of social service departments. She does this in the face of a district that employs the rhetoric of diversity and community service quite eloquently but rarely places resources, defines policy, or supports innovative programs that can make a difference. Catherine admits that much of the work to develop the school into a neighborhood service center has "come out of our hides!" The community-school coalition has written grants to support the programs, her teachers have rescheduled their days to open up space for needed public and adult-family services, and she and her administrative team have had to learn "creative budgeting!"

> A year and a half ago, I got a call that we [our school] were identified as a neighborhood service center. I said "What does that mean?" My supervisor said, "It means that you're going to be getting more resources. The police department will be sending a policeman to your school, and he'll be there on a daily basis and he'll be patrolling the neighborhood." We had been identified as a target school because our neighborhood crime rate was so high. Prior to this, the Garrett Park Neighborhood Association, which is our neighborhood association, and I had been in contact. I called them, and I said, "Can we meet, because we've been identified as a neighborhood service center and a police officer will be connected to us." We just thought that we had to identify what our needs were and what this neighborhood service center meant to us. We started a task force that met initially every 2 weeks and then once a month. Currently, the chairperson of the task force is from the neighborhood association.

I asked Catherine what prepared her for this job. She laughed loudly and said, "I don't know!" She admits that her upbringing didn't prepare her, as she led a sheltered life, attended Catholic private schools, lived in a suburban neighborhood, and had parents who were very strict: "I had unreasonable curfews, and I could not date until after high school." A little later in the same conversation, she recalled a critical moment in her early years of teaching that she felt probably set in motion her current advocacy for school and community linkages:

> I went to teach in the public school system because I wanted a teaching job. When I first walked into that class at Vernon L. Daly Junior High School, there was a girl named Paula. Back then, in 1977, I was really naive. Here this girl comes in, she's a seventh grader, and she comes into my class pregnant. That was a rude awakening for me. It was a different situation. One day I said to the principal, Mr. Hamlin, "Do you know that these kids are smoking marijuana in the bathroom? I walk by the bathroom during lunch time and there's smoke! Then they come into my class stoned!" And he said to me very calmly, "Catherine, if I walk in there, I can't prove it. They'll flush it down the toilet. And what do I say to the parents? Their parents will want to know how I have proof of it." This was all so new to me. I thought, why weren't we working with the parents? Why didn't we have people on campus who could help the kids? There was no support.

It was this experience and many others that have urged Catherine to create a school that links needed services to students and their families and that encourages parents to participate in the education of their children.

Creating Connections With Families

This intricate and powerful web of school and community that Catherine weaves with her administrative team, teachers, parents, and community leaders to address the needs of all children is reminiscent of her personal value for family and commitment to shift the way school people think about their work with "other" cultures.

> The family is very important! There is a closeness we all shared and a respect for the elders. I was born in Havana, Cuba. When I was little girl we lived with my grandmother and grandfather. When we came to the United States, there was a sense of loss. It's been 34 years, and I have not seen my grandmother . . . my

grandmother on my father's side. On my mother's side, my grandmother came over (to Florida) and we are close to her and my aunt. There is a big loss when, for political reasons, you don't see your family for years and years and years. We never chose to go back because there is a big fear that if our family went back to visit, something would happen to us because my father was involved in politics against Castro.

I spoke to my grandmother this summer [in 1994, after a 34-year separation]. One of the teachers at the elementary school went to Cuba because he was on a mission for the Seventh Day Adventist Church. He said that he would look her up. I sent her a little care package, and he did look her up and gave her the package. He brought back a video of my grandmother and two aunts. Just prior to him going, I was able to connect through a Canadian long-distance company. I called her up and I talked to her for 10 minutes, that's all the calling card allows you to do. I just talked with her last weekend again through the same Canadian connection. It's good to keep in contact. For years, I would try to call through the international operator, and they'd say, "You can't get through, you can't get though." Or, "There is no answer." I would write letters, and sometimes I would get letters back from her but otherwise I would get no response.

This theme of family is important in Catherine's professional work as she endeavors to include families by creating connections with early childhood and parenting associations, health agencies, and recreational programs. The importance of this theme is evidenced in regular staff development sessions that include learning about nontraditional families and domestic and internationally diverse peoples. Catherine is attentive to valuing the ethnic diversity among her teachers, staff, children and their families, and community members. One belief she stresses in her message to the school community is that the child should know and respect his or her own cultural heritage and language. Building on this self-pride is the first step to creating a learning environment in which children receive a solid academic education. Catherine shared how her own pride in her Cuban lineage had been developed:

I remember sitting in a reading group in second grade and being embarrassed to read. When the teacher called on you, you had to stand up and read. I can remember feeling really stupid and being called a "spick." I had some friends, so I wasn't ostracized, but I knew that I were different. My father said, "We're in this country, America, but you will not forget your language. We will speak Spanish in this home. And you are Cuban, so your values are Cuban." Being Cuban meant keeping your culture. When it came to growing up and becoming a teenager, there were certain things that you didn't do. You didn't stay out late, and you couldn't go out by yourself. Virginity played an important role. My mother never dated my father. Her father told my father how many days a week he could come visit his daughter: "You will come on Mondays, Wednesdays, and Fridays from 6 to 8. And you will sit in that chair and she will sit there, and at 8 o'clock, you'd best be on your way!" That was respect for self and respect and pride for your family. Family honor was very important. Also, keeping the language and your foods was an important part of culture. At the same time that we kept our culture, we were expected to learn English and this [American] system.

Catherine encourages teachers and children to talk openly about their ideas of "differences." Although some of the notions might be erroneous, often laden with negative stereotypes, she believes that getting these ideas on the table and addressing, correcting, and revising these thoughts can truly begin a more productive dialogue. Much of the art work, parenting activities, recreational programs, language classes, and community outreach is grounded on identifying misinformation regarding "others" and introducing interventions that correct perceptions. Catherine admits that relationships are not at a point of complete openness and that conversations still have a tenor of bias, but "it is a long, involved process to change images, but at least we've started."

Perhaps the most significant aspect of developing cultural pride is knowing one's language. Catherine believes that children can learn about their roots and who they are if they learn the beauty and heartbeat of their mother tongue. She also believes that children should learn the languages of other children because it adds to the child's own "global education. I believe it builds self-confidence knowing that you can learn anything you set out to learn, like another language." This point was brought home in a peculiar teaching situation:

I was hired as a bilingual teacher for the first grade, in Texas. I had Hispanic children that needed bilingual education, but I also had Caucasian children. I taught in Spanish and in English. The principal took me aside and said, "Don't teach those kids in Spanish because they need to learn English." That was part of her philosophy. I didn't do that. The strange thing about it was that we were in Texas. I just took it for granted that the parents of the kids who were Hispanic knew Spanish and wanted their children to learn or keep the Spanish language. So when they [the parents] came to conferences, I would speak to them in Spanish. Many of them, however, would look at me with an, "Are you crazy, lady?" sort of expression. Some of them really didn't know Spanish, others wanted me to speak to them in English, and the majority wanted their children to learn English and not speak Spanish in the classroom! Of course, there were some parents who appreciated what I was doing, but the majority had the same attitude as the principal. It was really sad.

Catherine is very critical of immigrants who come to the United States and do not keep their language and cultural traditions. She speaks harshly about those who choose total assimilation: "I believe they [immigrant parents] rob the following generations . . . of knowing the beauty and richness of their mother country." Although she believes that the children must be taught English and the U.S. governing system, "so that they can succeed in the new country," Catherine echoes her father's admonishment to her, "If you come to this country you have to learn English, but don't lose what and who you are—Cuban."

"This Is Not About Me or Them. It's About Children."

A tension on Catherine's web is her philosophy of leadership, which she believes conflicts with the actual practice and role expectations of school leaders in her district. Although she acknowledges that central-office administrators agree in a "goodness and integrity" clause, she finds that for her superiors, the rhetoric is used to mask activity and practice that is not focused on the "right things to do for children and their families." She explained,

Many times, our school leaders, no names please, ask, "Well, what's in it for me? Or, for my children's school?" This ideal we call public school is not for them or for me, it belongs to everyone in the community, and we are all responsible for what happens here. We all own this learning process.

Often frustrated by the attitudes of school administrators, tears filled her eyes as she said, "This is not about me or them. It's about children." Indeed, she admits that the teachers found it difficult to understand "my way of leadership, which is to have open discussions, make reasonable and fair decisions, and encourage everyone to step forward and be responsible for this learning community."

Catherine encourages every member of her learning community to define who he or she is as a person and a professional educator. It is through this reflective process that Catherine believes that people develop their own powers to stand up and choose to do what's right. She came to this understanding through a very personal conflict, a marital divorce. The divorce pressed her to question "who I was and what I stood for." She shared,

I feel like I was a late bloomer, but this taught me a lot about what I really needed in my life. First, I needed to live in a city where I could work in a school and make a difference, and I needed to have a family that had strong Catholic values.

As an elementary school principal, Catherine values teachers who are innovative and "are hardworking. I value a person who can stand up and be independent." This, she explains, is very important, especially in the challenging classrooms of an inner-city school.

I really think that teachers need to do everything they can to help and encourage the child. I had that kind of motivation. My sophomore year English teacher was the one who said, "You have some worth. You can write. You can do well in life." I was also in her journalism class and on the newspaper staff. When she got married, there was a group of us who went to her wedding; we were all on the newspaper staff together. Also, my senior year teacher, Mr. Fili, was a nontraditional teacher, as he taught in a manner that I had never experienced before. He made you really reflect and think in his English class. He took me aside one day, and he said, "Are you going to college?" And I said,

"Yeah." And he goes, "Well, because you should go to college." He made a point of saying that to me. I remember one time he returned one of my papers, and he put a big mark, "Do Over" on it. I was really insulted. I said, "What do you mean, do over?" (laughter) He said to me, "You can do better than that. Do it again." It was content. He just didn't think I had put enough thought into it. He was right! You know, if you expect more, you get more!

Because of these experiences and others like them, Catherine encourages teachers in the school to develop academically challenging and inclusive curriculum and instructional methods. Although remedial work in reading and writing is needed for most of the children attending the school, she believes and acts from the fundamental idea that all children can learn to think and to behave in positive ways if given the best tools. She explained that the value of hard work is a lesson that schools must teach children because many do not have the parental support at home. Many of her beliefs, such as hard work, have not sat well with teachers in the school. Catherine says, "They [the teachers] want it easy, so they make excuses for the children. You know, all the expected stereotypical and discriminatory comments. Those are not the teachers that children, any children, deserve." Hard work, perseverance, and fighting for one's beliefs coupled with the tenderness of family became the strong themes of Catherine's stories.

My grandmother used to sing to me nursery rhymes. I remember that. A lot of the stories I heard were about the family. Stories like how my mother's father came to Cuba on this little raft from Spain. He was a self-made man. My grandparents were originally from Spain and the Canary Islands. They came to Cuba with literally nothing, but with hard work, they succeeded. My father's family had very little, too, but my father worked hard to get an education. Our family lived comfortably in Cuba for several years, then Castro came.

In the beginning, I think, most Cubans were glad that Castro was coming about. As a little girl living in Santiago, which was by the mountains, I could hear the guns, the shooting as he [Castro] was in the mountains. He hadn't come down yet. He was doing his rebel rousing up there. One of the things that happened when I was a little girl was that I got very nervous and

upset about the shootings that I would hear. So I wasn't able to
sleep. We had this housemaid; she'd put me between the toilet
bowl and the wall. One time, there was a milk strike in Santiago,
so we had gone out to the farm to get some milk, and one of the
military planes started to shoot at our car. In 1960, my mother
and father, my sister, who was 2 months old, and myself, I was
5, came to the United States because of the political situation
with Castro. We went to Miami first for a few days, then we went
to New York City to settle. When we got to New York, it was the
beginning of the Castro regime, and there weren't a lot of Cubans there [New York]. My father had a difficult time getting a
job because "they" said, "You're from a banana country." That's
what a lot of employers said to my father. There was also the
feeling that "Castro is going to fall, and you're going to go back
to your country." My father had a hard time finding a job.

I believe that hard work and having a strong family and
community is the only way children can make it today, but most
of the time, I believe I'm the only one who is trying to do anything to build this support in our school district.

Over time, her belief in mutual respect and responsibility and
her passion for the work of schools to focus on creating dynamic
learning environments for all children began to take hold in her
school. Garnering the respect and support of her veteran faculty and
central office superiors, however, has not been easy.

The paradox that women of color, who take on leadership positions, face is that we want to make a difference, and everyone
says they want you to, but they don't give you any support. So,
from the outset, we don't see that we're any different from other
school leaders, but the reality is that we are different and that
scares people. I mean, I know I am an Hispanic woman, but I
never believed *that* was going to make the value of my efforts
less than anyone else. I know I'm equal, I know I'm capable.
That's how I got here. But it is my "self-confident attitude," my
fight for equity, that's seen as negative in this organization.
There's a backlash for being a leader with a different voice.

She tells, in her many stories of practice, that school leadership
is both cognitively and affectively thoughtful. Cognitive, because
leaders should always seek new knowledge. Affective, because

leaders must value relationships and reflexivity. As she continues to learn and practice her craft in a caring, nurturing, and knowledgeable manner, she continues to do what she feels is right. Because Catherine views herself as a

> learner and not the one who has all the answers, people question my ability as the school principal. We have to learn that we work as a team to lead schools ahead. I guess that's what gets me in trouble with the boys downtown (laughter)!

There is a struggle that many women face, that is, to weave their own web that is inviting and inclusive and embraces such characteristics of integrity as the value of family, the merits of open and candid networking, and the desire to address the different needs of children and their families. Their web is constantly censured by policy and action that seek to exclude and separate, battering the very spirit and integrity of the web. What Catherine is doing as a Latino woman, an elementary school principal, and advocate for minority children and their families is important. Because she weaves a web that genuinely links the school with its multiple communities, there are constant tangles that ensnare, entrap, and otherwise impede her work. In many ways, Catherine's battle is just beginning, but it is a battle I know she is prepared for.

Note

1. Catherine and I began our interview process early in the 1994-1995 school year; however, because of conflicting schedules, we were unable to resume our conversations for nearly 5 months. We completed our final three interviews at her school during a tumultuous period in her principalship. Since the completion of the interviews and the writing of this story, Catherine has found resolutions to many of the tensions she had been experiencing with her district office and immediate supervisor. In short, she has been able to construct her activities around a core of beliefs that places children first. During a recent informal visit to her school, teachers and parents commented to me that due to Catherine's philosophy and work to place children first, she has gained much respect and trust among teachers, parents, and community professionals.

5

Capturing the Soul— Working for Fellowship

Jackie's Story— An African American Woman

Jackie, short for Jacquilyn,[1] an African American woman, grew up in a predominantly White township outside a large metropolitan city in the Midwest. Her entry into the world of formal schooling and lifelong education began on the day she was born, but she cannot remember that far back. She begins wryly, "I'll start when I was 4." Her father, a respected teacher at a predominantly White junior high school, had a strong impact on her life. Going to work with her father was a moment that she spoke of in detail:

> My earliest memories of my father were his love for learning and love for me. My dad was a science teacher who later became a microbiologist. As a youngster, I remember visiting my father's ninth-grade science class. I remember the attention I received from his students. Before meeting his class, I remember vividly walking down the long hallway toward his classroom with my small hand in his. It made me feel I was in for a treat. I remember the dark green floor and the rows of narrow metal doors with locks on narrow silver handles. It was all so foreign, so intimidating, yet I felt protected.

Her father's love for learning, as shown in his classroom teaching, was also reflected in their family values. Jackie grew up in a family of six children, the third and oldest female child. She describes her mother as an intelligent, engaging, caring woman who was an outstanding role model. Jackie proudly reported that her mother was hired as the "first female, Black or White, inhalation therapist at a major university hospital." Just as Jackie's father valued formal schooling, her mother stressed the need for her children to learn to think:

> My mother, who valued learning, would engage us in games and puzzles that challenged our thinking and imagination. We had what seemed to be every board game invented. We had Scrabble, Monopoly, Sorry, Parcheesi, Checkers, Chinese Checkers, and many more. My mother enjoyed challenging us with three-dimensional puzzles you disassemble then put back together or nature puzzles with 500 pieces! My mother enjoyed these activities and would engage herself alongside us.

Jackie's father and mother also valued learning in an experiential environment. Learning meant respecting the earth by knowing it better. Her parents conveyed these values during family camping trips, nature hikes, and gardening. During the summer and fall months, many happy memories were built around the discovery of frogs, night crawlers, and snapping turtles and around hunts for walnuts and hickory nuts. Slowly, Jackie gained a genuine appreciation and awe for the miracles of Mother Nature.

On Being the Only Black Child in Class

The seasons always brought new discoveries, but the fall was Jackie's favorite season as it marked the start of a new school year and a time for reflection and new beginnings. Although Jackie and her brother were the only Black children in the neighborhood elementary school, she has "mostly happy thoughts" of her friends and her many artistic and academic accomplishments. She came to her first formal schooling experience prepared to learn, thirsty for new discoveries. What she would learn in her first critical experience would prepare her for future discriminatory situations. Jackie describes her first-grade experience as a low point because her teacher punished her unfairly and differently from the other [White] children.

> It was 1957; my family lived in an all-White neighborhood of low- to middle-income families. Naturally, the school I attended with my two older brothers was all White. I adored school; however, my first-grade teacher certainly did not adore me. I remember our strained relationship. She made me feel unwelcome. At the time, I couldn't say exactly what made me feel this way. Perhaps it was her initial reaction toward me when I entered her class. I later came to surmise, with much certainty, that my first-grade teacher was racist. Of course, at the time, I was far too young to label the attitude; nevertheless, I understood that I was being treated harshly and different. When a female student misbehaved, she had to put her head down on the desk. If the female student happened to be me, I was humiliated! I sat under a table or under the teacher's desk. In those days, we had strict dress codes. The girls wore dresses; therefore, the humiliation turned to discomfort. I remember the sting of the icy cold floors on my bare thighs. The feel of the cold, unforgiving tile floors sent chills up my spine and pronounced more punishment for me than I deserved.

This turbulent relationship with her first-grade teacher caused Jackie to become frustrated, at times, hurt and angry, but most of all, confused. She often wondered why, no matter how well behaved she was or how excellent her schoolwork, she had been singled out. Jackie began to dislike her full name (Jacquilyn) because it took so long to write it, and "it seemed that my other classmates could write their names faster." She even came to doubt her own abilities. If not for the genuine care of other teachers, Jackie believes that she might have become a mediocre student. The first teacher Jackie recalls who took the time to care for each child in the class was the art teacher. Whenever the children made something, the art teacher would always find "the marvelous in everyone's work." She would praise liberally, and she both respected and praised Jackie's work:

> I looked forward to art. One reason was that our regular teacher would leave the room, and the art teacher would be in charge.

When the art teacher strolled in the classroom with her cart of art materials, the whole atmosphere changed. The art teacher had a pleasant disposition. It seemed she looked for the good in everyone's work. She was not intimidating. She valued my efforts and would use my artwork as an example. My artwork was even showcased on bulletin boards in the school hallways.

Another example of a nurturing teacher was Mrs. Faiderbe, whom Jackie calls "my guardian angel." Mrs. Faiderbe, a second-grade teacher in the classroom next door, would always say a kind and encouraging word to Jackie on the many unpleasant days when she had been banished from the classroom to sit on the cold hallway floor. Mrs. Faiderbe would become Jackie's second-grade teacher.

Mrs. Faiderbe provided opportunities for me to develop pride in my schoolwork. My school performance was outstanding. I earned flawless report cards that displayed my academic achievements and excellent behavior. It was in that year, I believe, that I decided that I would become a teacher. My earlier experiences in my father's classroom, and my development in Mrs. Faiderbe's class, convinced me that I would become a teacher.

After her successful second-grade year, Jackie sought leadership roles in her classes and through the student council. Given her outstanding academic achievements, maturity, and high level of peer- and self-responsibility, the teachers selected her for the "service squad," an award for good citizenship. That experience taught her about self-pride, perseverance, and care for others, values that she would one day champion in her own classroom.

Living With Segregation in Junior and Senior High School

Another critical event in Jackie's formal schooling experience was entering racially diverse junior high and high schools. This was much more of a challenge than Jackie had anticipated. Initially, she lost many of her elementary school friends, who joined the White cliques. Jackie was also shunned by her new Black peers, who felt that she was from the "White" side of the tracks. She recounted this conflictual time passionately:

> Sixth grade was a turning point for me. The school district de-
> cided to bus students from an all-Black neighborhood to the
> school I was attending. Naturally, I thought this was great! But I
> noticed a change in my White classmates, especially toward me.
> One of my best friends admitted that it was "OK" when it was
> only me, but she didn't like the idea of more Black students in-
> vading our class. I felt it didn't matter what color people were,
> but of course, it did matter, especially in junior high. I was totally
> ostracized by the White students with whom I went to elemen-
> tary school. Race started to become a major issue with me. The
> Black students, whose friendship I ached for, knew that I had not
> attended their school, and therefore, they viewed me as "up-
> pity." I did not like that label because that just wasn't my per-
> sonality.

During these delicate years of adolescence, the importance of belonging to a group is crucial to one's self-identity and esteem, but
Jackie found herself left out. Not belonging created within her a
sense of despair and loneliness because "I couldn't connect with anyone." Her self-esteem bruised, Jackie turned her attention to her
schoolwork and sought mentorship from supportive adults, such as
her science teacher and the assistant principal. Because she had few
friends, she simply wanted to go on without being noticed; however,
her adult mentors expected a lot more from Jackie.

> After much prodding and encouragement by my 7th-grade sci-
> ence and homeroom teacher, I entered the schoolwide science
> fair. I won second place! I also entered the schoolwide speech
> contest and tried, unsuccessfully, to recite from memory *The Cre-
> ation* by James Weldon Johnson. These experiences, and many
> others, challenged me to move out of my comfort zone, helped
> me realize my own potential, and prepared me for future chal-
> lenges.

Jackie became keenly aware of the segregation within her school.
Invisible yet very real boundaries crisscrossed the lunch room,
clearly defining color, gender, disability, and sexual identification.

These walls were supported by student attitudes and behavior that were often confrontational, serving to demean and objectify. Jackie worked to develop understanding and respect among her peers, but she could not find the delicate tools needed to unravel the mythologies of difference.

> Even though I did not have any close relationships with my school peers, I had for the most part gained their respect. On one-on-one relationships and interactions within the classroom environment, I felt fine. I could relate, get along, and work with just about anyone in class. I knew from this experience that we [i.e., all the students] had the capacity to get along, but there were too many superficial walls that prevented positive interactions. What could *I* do?

A heavy pause followed this query, during which I felt that Jackie, in her mind's eye, had parted a veil. With deep intensity, Jackie shared that this had been the beginning of an important crossing for her. She realized that she lived in both a private place of self-affirmation and courage and a public place that was oppressive and hopeless. Traversing both had seemed all too ludicrous to her and so she longed for a place of harmony, a community of mutual respect. In high school, all the lessons learned about perseverance, developing one's knowledge and skill, and reaching for the stars seemed like old clothes two sizes too small. The pressures to fit in found her floundering in a sea of mediocrity. She remembers that she didn't want to be identified by her peers as a "goody-two-shoes" or labeled as being "too smart."

> Fortunately, my attempt to transform myself into one of the group was short-lived. I just couldn't just get by. I realized that I was hurting myself, and I didn't like that. This lesson, of never letting yourself down, is one that I have cherished and pressed upon every young person I have come in contact with since.

This, Jackie reflects, is when she crossed the bridge of mediocrity and decided that her personal and private text would guide her steps. She didn't care much for the notion of "letting yourself down and losing all self-integrity and responsibility." She also knew that when a person does not "work to become all they could become," she or he would become "unfulfilled and dissatisfied with one's personal endeavors." Reflecting on her own schooling and that which she stands for in her practice today, Jackie wrote in her journal:

> Even though I attended integrated schools, unfortunately for me and for my White classmates, we were still taught from a segregated curriculum. We were taught nothing of the contributions made by people of non-European descent. Over the years, we as African Americans have been conditioned, along with our White counterparts, to respect the contributions made by those Americans of European descent. It is equally vital that all children learn and respect the contributions made by African Americans and other ethnicities, such as Native and Asian Americans. Segregated curriculum harms White students because it breeds a false sense of superiority and distorts their perceptions of themselves and others and denigrates all the others by breeding a myth of insignificance.
>
> The questioning of myself, as to who I was, became stronger in high school and my college years. As a result of this lack of attention to the uniqueness of the African American citizen, I was an underachiever. I knew I could have done better. I felt cheated.

On Being a Black Woman in the 1960s

Jackie continues to speak out against the exclusion of difference in the formal schooling curriculum. She shares that this social consciousness and deep sense of collective responsibility was "truly awakened during the civil rights movement, the time of Malcolm X, the Vietnam War, rhythm and blues music, and protest marches." The 1960s, she recalls, was, for the most part, a great political and social struggle in which a singular, elite society was challenged by the diverse values and needs of the oppressed. At this time of her life, Jackie learned to articulate her personal voice through the lyric moods of poetry. She shared a personal writing:

> The years between 1965 to 1969 was a period of awakening. I believe for the first time that I began to understand my need for community, unity. Many of the events in the sixties have shaped my life, so many that I can only relate it in a poem, a montage:

A short sketch of the 1960s requires magnanimous
     reflections
For the '60s depicts many complexities of a pluralistic
     society.
Looking through the lens of an African American,
The '60s provide a collage of memorable events.
It was an era that began with hope in the form of President
     Kennedy.
It ushered in the great works of Dr. Martin Luther King,
And the many unsung heroes of the movement for racial
     equity.
It was a time of Viola Liuzzo. And it fueled the spirit of the
     Freedom bus rides throughout the deep South.
It was nearly a decade of Robert Kennedy and the antics of
     Jimmy Hoffa.
A time when our country was under siege by J. Edgar
     Hoover.
It was the time for the intrepid Malcolm X.
The '60s was the Motown sound, classic melodies of urban
     Detroit.
A belief in Huey P. Newton and the birth of the Black
     Panther Party.
It was James Brown proclaiming, "Say it loud! I'm Black
     and I'm Proud!"
It's Mohammed Ali "flying like a butterfly and stinging like
     a bee."
The '60s were bell bottoms, dashikis, afros and afro puffs.
It's when television discovered "Julia." Yes, the first
     prime-time television program with a
     professional-single mother of color.
It's when mainstream, White America discovered that Black
     Americans had a voice,
and the Black Americans expected that voice to be heard.
The '60s exposed Mississippi, Alabama, and Arkansas as
     dens of racial inequity, yet allowed northern states to
     hide behind the hypocrisy of integration.
Sadly the nation witnessed the assassination of four great
     men.
It was the riots of Watts and Detroit.
The '60s were peculiar as it polarized the races with forced
     busing, and yet enabled a liberal consciousness.

It nurtured strange dichotomies forcing people apart yet
    encouraging diverse people to come together.
This was a time of the hippie, the militant, the silent
    majority,
the draft-dodger, the sit-ins and walk-outs, and the Vietnam
    War.
It was a time to protest and burn bras, a time to boycott.
The '60s challenged the "establishment" to include the law,
    and the schools.
After sifting through these many events, the locus for me
    becomes clear.
The events of the '60s was a cry for basic human respect.
The need to feel respect, to be treated with dignity.

Her sense of equity and desire to share with others the need for
understanding became her war chant. Jackie had learned to be tough
and tender, to be smart and courageous.

How Does One
Become a "Good Teacher"?

One of the few African American students from her high school
to go on to college, Jackie attended a large state university, earning a
bachelor of science degree in elementary education with a specialty
in physical education and integrative creative arts. Armed with her
newly earned teaching certificate, she was reluctant to enter the
teaching ranks. Jackie came face-to-face with an expectation that she
had unknowingly created. Throughout her many formal years of
schooling, Jackie had subconsciously stored away all the qualities of
"good teaching."[2] Good teaching, as her stories indicate, emphasized caring, thoughtfulness, and creativity. A good teacher established an environment in which all children could learn; encouraged
self-respect; and built a positive community based on honesty, trust,
teamwork, and respect. After sharing many stories and examples of
good teaching, Jackie said,

When I earned my teaching certificate, I didn't want to teach. I
didn't feel ready to take on what seemed to be an insurmount-
able task, teaching. I began to remember the suffering of stu-

dents at the hands of a teacher and the effects of peer pressure. Michael Oakeshott [1960] asserts that the mind is made of perceptions, recognitions, thoughts of all kinds, emotions, sentiments, affections, deliberations, and purpose, and of actions which are responses to what is understood to be going on. Now that I had my teaching certificate, I didn't feel I understood the pedagogy necessary to be a good teacher and didn't have the skills to deal with the complex lives and minds of young children.

So overwhelmed by the responsibility of teaching, Jackie enrolled in an MA program in radio and television education. Her first professional job at a large university's Instructional Television Department challenged her to creatively teach subject matter using the visual media. She recalls that she was intrigued by communication technology and its potential for enhancing teaching and learning. Her work in developing innovative training videos affirmed that she "could be a good teacher."

Jackie entered the K-12 classroom because "teaching was a big part of me . . . and I felt confident, after some time to reflect on my work, that I could set up an environment of self-respect, respect for diversity, and collective responsibility." Jackie's successes in instructional television convinced her that she had the ability to go beyond the information-giving model of learning toward a learning environment that gave students "the confidence to explore."

It was 4 years after my graduation that I was drawn back to the classroom. Once I got there, I fell in love with teaching. It was time to do my part. To make my students feel special and help them to set and attain their goals.

Jackie returned to the school district from which she had graduated and was hired as a sixth-grade teacher by one of her former school principals. She has been a teacher there for 16 years. Although Jackie knows that young people today constantly hear negative messages that evoke feelings of hopelessness and irresponsibility, she believes that these messages can be reversed—if youth feel that they are in turn "respected and are made to feel special." If she had learned anything from her experience in the first grade, it was just that. She added that she makes an effort to praise every child every day, to acknowledge each individual's work, and to respect and call for student contributions and participation in class activities and lessons. At every opportunity, Jackie says that she stresses academic achievement, and she admits she sounds a bit "preachy" when it comes to the virtues of education. Preparing a curriculum proposal that advocated the need to build a community of leaders among eighth graders, she wrote in her journal,

> Clearly, educators working with adolescents must address their needs for personal growth and development. I agree with Dryfoos [1990] that schools must provide experiences that provide opportunities for healthy adolescent development. She contends that school-based interventions curricula are necessary in assisting adolescents in making healthy life choices, such as experiences in problem solving, social skills and moral reasoning. I believe the "other" adolescents, those not considered moderately or severely at-risk, need the same opportunities in personal growth and development in an educational setting as well. All children can benefit from such educational opportunities that are designed to develop personal skills in problem solving, social awareness and moral reasoning.

The importance of the teacher as guide is reflected in Jackie's normal teaching day. Usually, she arrives in her classroom at 7:45 a.m., 15 minutes before the arrival of her first students. Jackie is well-groomed in her professional dress with matching accessories and shoes. She admits that her students think she is a "fine dresser," and that, she whispers, "is quite a compliment coming from sixth graders." She sets up the morning activities that include, she is "embarrassed to say, worksheets and other materials." As the students enter, she either talks with individuals or small groups. The conversation ranges from yesterday's activities to their families, morning adventures, and their studies. Students ask to help her, and she provides them with such duties as running errands, erasing or writing on the board, setting out learning tools, and straightening up the classroom.

"Fussing"

The bell rings promptly at 8:00 a.m., and a new day begins. Jackie smiles as she reflects on the start of a new day, "It's time for business!

The students know it. My principal used to say that I ran my class like a business." Although Jackie is embarrassed by that description of her class, she takes pride in being very organized and providing students the structures that "this age, puberty, need." Within her structured day and the class rules of behavior, students are provided ample opportunity to actively participate in learning while developing a positive, healthy, and open relationship with their teacher. For example, while the students begin their morning assignments, Jackie takes care of the basic logistics of roll, lunch, and generally "fussing at" the students. This fussing is Jackie's way of communicating her care and "mothering" of her young students.

> It was my way of sharing affection. They knew I cared when I fussed. I fussed at them for almost anything. I would say, "Robert, a gentleman wouldn't say that. He would say this." I would tell the girls with boyfriends that they were much too young. I would get after them about how their work was presented. I would fuss at them about how they sat at their desks. I would fuss if they didn't have their work done or if they weren't sitting straight in their chairs, or sometimes trivial concerns I might have. And the students seem to enjoy all my fussing.

Although this bantering might sound authoritarian and negative, Jackie's tone and demeanor is respectful, witty, and loving. Each child responds positively to her reminders, working tirelessly to produce his or her best work. Jackie's conversations with individual students, whether corrective or praising, were invariably at the student's level, eye to eye, with her hand on their arm or shoulder in a comforting, supportive gesture. Of the many teaching models in Jackie's experience, she has consciously chosen to emulate those emphasizing care and respect:

> As an educator, I believe one of my greatest challenges in working with adolescents is helping them to see and develop their inner capabilities; to help them recognize their inner strengths and talents. From my experiences as a classroom teacher, and from my personal life experiences and self-growth and development through various experiential-learning initiatives, I believe strongly in Sophie Haroutunian-Gordon's [1991] assertion that teaching is turning the soul, which I take to mean directing the

students toward objects that draw out the vision or understanding they already possess, thanks to their experience in the world. As an educator, I have a moral obligation to provide as many opportunities as I can to assist, guide, and direct students to "look where they should," thereby having a better chance of becoming productive members of society.

A Teacher Who Loves Children

Coupled with her firm belief that children must be treated with respect is her dogged belief that all children can learn and excel. She has organized her day into five units that begin with reading, followed by math, science, language arts, and social studies. In each of these segments, students are actively involved in reading silently and aloud and answering and posing questions, both orally and on paper. In the reading unit, Jackie begins the lesson with an experience drawn from real life that is in some way related to the story to be read that day. This activity of allowing students to read aloud and to answer questions orally can be terrifying for the shy or unsure. Consequently, she expects students to support, not belittle, one another, and she exhorts them to embrace and try things they thought impossible to do.

Math time is a high activity time, with some students doing problems on the chalkboards, other students at their desks doing individual assignments, and still others in groups or with Jackie. "Students are at different levels in math," explained Jackie, so she had the students working on a variety of activities. Choice is introduced into the lesson as the students can decide to do their math assignment in class or for homework. If they choose to take their work home, the students can select to participate in other constructive learning activities made available to them during this period. Jackie spends much of her time monitoring, helping individuals or groups of students, and redirecting student activities, "helping them to make choices." Although she had presented the lesson for the day at the start of this period, the students took charge of their learning, adding the lesson of self-responsibility.

It is not surprising that science is a special time in Jackie's classroom. She admits that her instructional methods have improved over time:

My science program (along with math) was pretty much text-book, paper, pencil, filmstrip, video, et cetera. I knew I had to change my teaching style. I wanted student learning to be more interactive, authentic and meaningful enough to encourage self-generated inquiry, self-stimulated knowledge. I learned about project-based science, which is a curriculum centered around driving questions and engages students in teamwork and dis-covery learning. . . . As I reflect back to the beginning of my use of this method, I know how crucial the teacher is to opening the doors of students' minds, to spark a desire, a need to see the relevancy, ignite an interest and provoke an awareness.

Her respect and care for the earth is evident in how she has struc-tured her lessons to coincide with the seasons. The lessons are filled with challenging questions that encourage children to think and dis-cover. She also employs computers, videos, pictures, charts, and many visual aids that guide them through their learning process—a throwback, she admits, to her creative art days and her work in tech-nology. Beginning with the exploration of the ecosystem, students begin to appreciate how fragile the earth is. They learn about soil and plants, study the weather and the solar system, then move on to an investigation of energy and matter. "It is important that my students learn that everything in this world, including humans, is linked to-gether," explains Jackie. Her lessons later in the year include the in-troduction of the periodic element chart, which she admits she does not favor,[3] and a unit on the human body and maturation process, which she feels is a ripe area for questions and new discoveries. "Hu-man maturation causes a lot of silliness among adolescents," laughs Jackie. She points out that it is difficult at this age to be "mature, so, I have to remind them to be respectful, not be silly, and try to learn about human growth and development."

Language arts is admittedly Jackie's weakest subject area. Cur-rently, this period is filled with worksheets and book work, with an emphasis on proper grammar and writing skills. "Writing has not been one of my strong points," admits Jackie. "I know I need to really work on this so that my students' work in this area improves." Jackie has been working on developing activities in her language arts unit that promote critical thought, collaborative learning, and open dis-course around different ideas and feelings.[4] She laments the fact that in many of her school experiences, she was never allowed the opportunity to share her ideas, question her own and classmates' ideas, even debate the teachers.

> As an educator, my thinking about student learning has changed over time. At one time, I did what I had been taught and ob- served: gave information. Teachers need to be willing to allow for more student discourse, more time for discovery and the ex- change of ideas and new learnings with one another. You know the concept *less is more?* I internalized this to mean to give less time on lecturing and doling out facts and more time to students seeking out knowledge on their own through collaboration, in- quiry, formulation of questions and ideas, constructive dialogue, and cooperative learning. I am not afraid of challenges or step- ping out of my comfort zone anymore. But, this is a big step for me! I feel that I can succeed and that my students can benefit from new learning experiences . . . in spite of my own apprehen- sions [about my abilities].

Social studies ends the day with a course of study that often leaves the students excited about learning. At the beginning of the year, Jackie teaches map skills, then moves on to ancient civilizations and world cultures that takes the students first to the Middle East and across all the continents. The students' journey from one conti- nent to another provides an opportunity for Jackie to tell new stories and introduce foreign traditions, customs, and beliefs. It is a time "when I can open their minds to understand and appreciate other people." Perhaps Jackie's goal to establish an understanding and empathetic community is most evident in this unit.

> I was especially fond of teaching sixth-grade social studies be- cause it was on world cultures. This was one venue where I was able to model appreciation for the contributions of ancient and present-day world cultures. I worked hard to make my students aware of the impact of the Mesopotamian era, ancient Egypt, Greek and Asian societies, India's uniqueness and Gandhi's in- tegrity, and the multiplicities of the people and geography of the vast African continent. The beauty of the various continents and their diverse populations was my theme.
>   I then tried to relate this world scope to the United States. I seized the celebrations on Martin Luther King's birthday to be-

gin to make connections. I had my students memorize and recite the first sentence of the second paragraph of the Declaration of Independence that reads, "I hold these truths to be self-evident, that all men are created equal, that they are endowed by their Creator with certain inalienable Rights, that among these are Life, Liberty and the Pursuit of Happiness." We examined the meaning of key words and phrases and discussed what they meant in a global way. This exchange was one of my high points in teaching because I was making moral ideas more relevant, more real, to their personal lives. We would discuss the Civil Rights Movement, the Vietnam War, and women's rights. Sixth graders are such a delightful group of learners to have this discourse with because they are so candid. It was encouraging to be in the midst of 10- to 12-year-old White, Black, and Brown beautiful faces who were discussing issues that affect the pursuit of happiness of all people. This is what I believe teaching is all about, making these moral connections.

Jackie believes that, as a child, she brought to the classroom a desire to learn and a "wealth of information." Because many of her teachers were able to link the knowing she brought with their curriculum content, Jackie's desire for new discoveries grew. This seed has nourished Jackie's own belief that the teacher's moral commitment is to embody the excitement and usefulness of learning, and that the teacher's actions must stretch and surprise and open new doors for all students. She writes,

> School is the place where wonderful and exciting challenges for children's growth and development should happen. The teacher is gatekeeper. In spite of the negative experiences I encountered, I had a strong determination to learn and a sense that I was special. My dad taught me that. All children need teachers who believe in them, so that they [the children] can excel. Teachers are the movers and the shakers of a better world.

Believing that teachers have a moral responsibility toward the success of their young charges, Jackie's care and commitment are clearly reflected in her interactions with individual children. She can sometimes sound like the sidewalk preacher extolling the virtue and value of education. Often, she would share her tumultuous school experiences to encourage children to apply themselves in their academic endeavors.

> They [the children] were very clear about where they came from [a blue-collar neighborhood]. They knew that it was expected by society that they'd really do no better than that. But in my class, they knew that I didn't believe that. I would share my story about underachieving, living up to mediocre expectations. I would teach the children not to lower their standards!

Jackie tells the story of two children, Gina and Donny, two children who could have fallen through the cracks of an uncaring system. Gina, a Native Amerindian-Caucasian child, was bubbly, cute, and well-liked by her peers. She was also very bright, worked diligently in class, did her homework, and earned high marks; however, the peer pressure of adolescence affected her. Wanting to belong to the group, she began to display nonproductive classroom behavior, such as excessive talking and "simply goofing-off," which distracted her from doing her schoolwork. Jackie remembers how she had to confront Gina often about her "inappropriate" talking in class and finally had to sit Gina down for a private talk. Much of their discussion included Jackie sharing her own stories about growing up. Over time, Jackie relates that Gina began to find a balance between her need to be part of a group and her own self-respect and desire to learn. Recently, Jackie found out that Gina, now in college, is studying to become a teacher.

Donny had been a challenge for Jackie; he had come to her classroom with a range of personal problems. Because Donny was physically larger than his peers, most classmates kept their distance, which Donny often used to instigate occasional disturbances. Jackie says of Donny, "He seemed to always have a chip on his shoulder. But he was always respectful toward me." He was a bright kid but because of the unsettling turmoil in his young life, he put little effort into his schoolwork. Jackie spoke extensively about her one-on-one conversations with Donny, and although he never became an honor student in middle school, his current high school teachers have told Jackie that he is performing well academically and is respected by his peers.

Jackie's formal school experience taught her that she had to let her students know that she cared about them. This meant that she would be very clear with the children about her expectations, both academic and social. She had to treat each child fairly and be available if a child needed extra support. One school year, Jackie's ability to develop empathy, understanding, and respect in her classroom was challenged by a new student. This young girl, Jackie recalls, was physically disabled: "She was pretty tough, and she was very much on the defensive about having one arm. In fact, she even started fights over her arm. She had a lot of anger over her physical disability." Not knowing what to do, Jackie fell back on her own sense of equity and decided that this young child would not be treated any differently from the other children. Jackie decided that she would be direct, make her academic and behavior expectations clear, and hold the young girl to her standards. Initially, a bit of a power struggle transpired, but as Jackie retells the event, "She knew what I expected. I put it on her to decide, to be responsible for her own work and her own behavior. There were no excuses!" Apparently, addressing the young girl's attitude proactively helped the entire class develop respect for one another, regardless of differences. At the end of the school year, Jackie recalled that the young girl was appreciative that she had been treated fairly and "no different from anyone else."

As Jackie writes and reflects on both her formal schooling experiences and her work as a teacher, she clearly communicates a sense of pride and power and a conviction that she can create a community that values care, trust, respect, choice, teamwork, and faith:

> The learner must feel special and that he or she has significant contributions to make to our society. As the teacher, I must afford each child many opportunities to develop and discover new knowledge in a safe and nurturing environment. In addition, to feel comfortable to present his or her contributions. In this way, it's helping children become lifelong learners. Helping students to take charge of themselves so that they realize that they have immense power within them. There are many avenues through which the educator can guide and direct learning. But it is the art and science of teaching to create the total climate, the learning environment.

Jackie continues her work toward developing a community of respect and self-affirmation in her classroom—an environment, she assures me, that provides children with an opportunity to discover their own identity and form positive relationships with others. Because she believes that power and achievement come from a soul that is confident and gracious, she pushes her students to work hard and face challenges with vigor. This notion that every student must also be responsible for his or her learning process builds self-reliance and empathetic relations. These are the important lessons in Jackie's classroom community:

> Adolescents, high-risk or not, need learning opportunities that "turn the soul," opportunities that develop inner capabilities, strengths, and talents. I, as an educator, am compelled to seek out ways for students to learn beyond the traditional ways of learning. That is, learning that draws from within the students' personal experiences and knowledge, that relies on intrinsic capabilities, that requires students to be responsible for their individual academic growth and development and that is responsive to other human beings.

In addition, Jackie is committed to a curriculum that is ethnically diverse, inclusive, global, and empowering. The themes around which she builds her lessons are grounded in leadership, service, respect, and teamwork. In a journal entry, Jackie's comments clearly reflect her continued learning and purpose as an educator.

> For years, African Americans were expected to embrace and excel in a curriculum that excluded their contributions to national and world events. I was disheartened by the recent D-Day observances presented by the major television networks. My father and uncles served during that time. My mother and aunt worked in the plants that manufactured goods for the military, and yet I saw very little to total omission of the African American contribution.
>
> What does this say to young children? This perpetuates misinformation and only incites further lack of respect for people of non-European descent. This blocks understanding and appreciation, and further complicates efforts toward harmonious existence. As an educator, I must continue to fight harder to ensure true understanding. Education has a moral purpose! Its purpose is to make a difference in the lives of all

students, to help them develop self- and other-respect so that they can live in a productive community, in an increasingly complex world.

Jackie's current work in the classroom speaks volumes against the ramifications of constant oppression viewed by children and youth on today's television. She claims that her first-grade experience, the racist attitudes of both Black and White peers during her middle and high school years, and her awareness of civic responsibility, highlighted by the events of the late 1950s and throughout the 1960s, has fueled her advocacy today. As we talked about her teaching, Jackie became enraged as she described television's lack of attentiveness to issues of racism and difference. She admonished television for its narrow images of diverse peoples and its often one-sided perspective of history. Jackie admits that she now carefully examines textbooks used at her school: "I don't use any that are racist or sexist!" She has also begun to teach students how to become "critical consumers of the print and visual media." This past school year, Jackie developed and taught a leadership program that employed experiential learning and provided multiple opportunities for students to learn and discuss current pressing social issues. She noted, "Critical dialogue among young people is important, and I'll be doing more with it this year." A piece of this experience will include the viewing of news programs, sitcoms, commercials, and movies with a keen eye toward stereotypic racist and sexist situations and conversations. After viewing the videos, students discuss and formulate arguments in letters to television producers, consumer advocate groups, and government officials.

Reflection: Jackie's Growth

Over the past 2 years of my work with Jackie, I have observed her dynamic and articulate advocacy against racism blossom. After I reviewed a letter she planned to send off to a national broadcasting agency, I jokingly said, "I've created a monster!" She quickly reprimanded me saying, "You've stretched me! That's good! You've made me feel that it's okay to say what I truly believe is right."

Two such instances of her struggle against racism in the media are illustrated in the following letters she had written to the producer of the "Good Morning America" program.

January 10, 1994. "Good Morning America" is in a position to present strong effective messages to seriously begin to eradicate the attitudes of racism. The ravages of racism is not just a conditioning of individual attitudes; its many forms permeate institutions and structures of the American society and the behaviors of its public officials, including the private sector as well.

Why can't . . . Charlie Gibson and Joan Lunden share their upbringing to illustrate the subtleties of racism and the effects on them and their families? . . . White discourse on White racism among such influentials as Barbara Walters, Ted Koppel, Peter Jennings, Diane Sawyer, George Will, Sam Donaldson is long past due and would no doubt send a strong and provocative message. This dialectic could begin an open and honest examination of racism.

In the beginning of this century, W. E. B. DuBois said, " . . the problem of the twentieth century is the problem of the colour line" (1903). We are now approaching the end of this century and this country is still suffering from disparaging race relations. . . . What more can minority groups say about racism that we have not said before? When will we really talk about institutionalized racism?

July 21, 1994. After the segment on the 1969 moon landing, the question was asked, "Where were you 25 years ago, July 20, 1969?" This question caused me to think, for 1969 was a significant time for me. It was a year of hope. It was a year for new beginnings. I was preparing to go to college and was eager to learn more about myself in a society that has so long denied many people of my color opportunities in education, housing, and employment. . . . The historical excerpt presentation that was centered around the 1969 moon landing failed miserably in capturing the essence of the '60s. Did the producer forget the social injustices of rampant racism during that time? And what did the producers mean during that montage of events that the TV show "Julia" made us more socially aware? Who were the "us" and what were the "us" made socially aware of?

How could Charlie Gibson say that the moon landing made "everyone" proud? There is no doubt that the space program is worth commemorating, but at the time, there were many citizens of this country living with the atrocities of racism that affected their living conditions and their quality of life. Who among them were proud of the moon landing?

In retrospect, Jackie attributes her beliefs and actions to her constant quest to learn more about herself, about teaching and learning, and about children. Growing up in a family that valued education and being touched by schoolteachers throughout her formal academic years provided a base from which Jackie has been inspired to create new and challenging learning venues and experiences for her students. Jackie wrote, toward the end of her interviews with me, that she had "no doubt that the leadership academies" and her continued education "has had a direct impact on how I view myself as a teacher and as a learner." She concluded, in a recent e-mail message to me,

I want to broaden my philosophy of community, community of learners. My teaching methods now include strategies that help my students become lifelong learners. Sometimes, I don't know how I'm going to get my students there, but I feel it is my moral obligation, as their teacher, to help, to guide them to become more responsible for their own learning and for one another.

Notes

1. All the names, with the exception of Jackie (Jacquilyn) are pseudonyms. It was Jackie's choice to use her name.

2. I probed a bit further, asking Jackie to define "good teacher." What I learned was that as a researcher, I should never expect a short, to-the-point response. Jackie found that telling me stories about good teachers and their works and providing me with examples of her work that she considered good teaching was the only way she could define good teaching.

3. I found Jackie's dislike for certain components of her curriculum interesting. Asking her why she disliked the periodic chart, she simply said that "in life, there are things that you like more than

other things." Truthfully, she admitted, she found it personally difficult to get too excited about the chart.

4. It is important to mention, at this point, that since the interviews, Jackie has worked hard to improve her writing skills and to
develop a more interdisciplinary approach to teaching language
arts. She no longer employs worksheets but uses diverse stories, current events, video, and recordings, which she integrates with writing
in different genres (i.e., short story, poetry, informative writing, and
editorial commentary).

6

I Won't Back Down

Jolie's Story—
An African American Woman

We must re-create an attractive and caring attitude in our homes and in our worlds. If our children are to approve of themselves, they must see that we approve of ourselves. If we persist in self-disrespect and then ask our children to respect themselves, it is as if we break all their bones and then insist that they win Olympic gold medals for the hundred-yard dash. Outrageous.

—Maya Angelou (1993, p. 103)

What I remember most of the many hours I spent with Jolie was how humbled I felt by her dogged individualism. Her speech is colored with bold strokes of strength, a deliberate cadence, and a sharp, sometimes biting, wit. The stories she told were reminiscent of children's story hour at the local library, where one world adventure after the next floods the air. Perhaps the best way to introduce Jolie is in her own words:

> I was born in a major urban city and attended mostly parochial schools. I'm your typical introvert person. Thinking, sensing, perceptive person. I got in trouble with that. I grew up in a

family of extroverts. They were a feely, touchy type of people—I was just the opposite. Part of my growing up is always somewhat being the opposite of them. I've always been quiet, reserved, and conservative.[1]

Jolie's self-portrait became an interesting study in opposites. On one hand, she defined herself as a "loner" and "a pretty good candidate to become a hermit."

I am very set in my ways, and, one of the things I have found of late, I was becoming a recluse. It's very comfortable. Currently, I go home and to my three dogs who greet me and I give them all hugs and kisses. I let the little guys out and they all come back in. We'll sit on the floor and play for about 5 minutes, then I turn on the music I like. I was really getting into it. I think I can easily become a recluse. Go to work, go to school, do my history and my reading and reports, and deal with the outside world infrequently. Now that's sort of ironic because I want to be involved.

A Sojourner

Yet there are many examples in Jolie's life that find her in the middle of the river, traveling to new places, and often paddling against the current. She explained that throughout her life, she has had to be clear with people about

who I am and am not. They have these conceptions that I must be married, have children, be loud and aggressive. . . . It's both a gender and color issue, I believe. . . . I am not married and my three dogs are my children. I am pretty no-nonsense and I tell people this.

This individual spirit, feisty energy, and resolve drove her youthful passion to "see the world." She shared,

I grew up in Detroit. As a child, it would cost you 25 cents to go from one end of the city to the other on the bus. I can remember going through different neighborhoods, different cultures. I remember being on the bus in my neighborhood going clear over to Eastern Market. Going through the Polish neighborhood,

Swedish, and going to Hamtramak. Then I'd get on another bus and head out to 8-mile, East Detroit, and I'd go through the Italian neighborhood and get to Assumption Grotto Catholic Church.

She was spirited as she spoke about the architectural wonders that distinctly marked each ethnic neighborhood. Jolie described the community churches, the corner stores, the people, the children, the schools, the many novel sites and smells that reflected the uniqueness of each community. This early introduction to different cultures and different people sparked Jolie's passion to know others, to travel and learn the histories of foreign lands. I was struck by this same tenacity later in her life when she told of a trip to the Berlin Wall, where she chipped a piece of the wall—"before they tore it down"— she added. Many of her stories revealed her thirst for discovery, for immersing herself in other cultures, and for going beyond her hermit's cottage. She made me laugh when she shared,

Whenever I go some place, I hate organized tours. I'd like to get out on my own. Don't tell me when I have to be back, just let me do what I want to do. The things I want to look at and discover are not necessarily on tours . . . like I went to Hawaii and I said, Don Ho!? Let's see something real!

Her desire for unique cultural experiences has strengthened her personal and professional commitment to multicultural education, that is, to broaden students' appreciation of others and to create a depth of understanding about "self." "I believe," Jolie shared, "that kids need to learn about their own background, which gives self-pride *and* at the same time grow to respect other individuals' histories" [emphasis added by Jolie]. At the time of our interviews, Jolie worked in an inner-city middle school where she was the department chair of the counseling department, counselor for the eighth-grade class, and summer school principal for the high school. The undersong of her many stories laments the lack of attention schools give to youth whose families are suffering from social and economic ills:

You know, I try to develop a sense of hope every day. I do that by modeling a positive behavior. Part of my nurturing of them is to help them develop into independent thinkers. We're running a school where we're not allowing the kids to think! I'm learning that these eighth-grade kids have not been taught to be responsible for their own learning in a school environment. Now, these kids are responsible because many of them have to take care of younger siblings, they have to cook, and some of them have to take care of their own parents. I have a child now who has spent most of her life taking care of a manic-depressive mother and calling the police every time her mother doesn't take her medication and gets violent.

Jolie was passionate as she explained that many of her students, mostly African American or of Hispanic heritage, had little understanding of the world, little desire to discover the richness of different cultures, and much less hope and control of their own lives:

I'm really working hard with my eighth graders because they're heading for high school. They need to take care of themselves and believe in themselves. That's where this idea of control comes in—feeling right with yourself. I had a young lady in today, and I said to her, "I know that life this year has been really crappy for you. Your parents are divorcing. Your mom is on your case and you're on her case. You've been skipping school and doing a whole lot of other things. You're a bright student, but you feel your life is crappy!" I told her that if she wanted to change things, she just had to choose to do it. There is a unique academic opportunity she can choose to participate in. The program offers her the support to complete high school, go to community college, and then into an engineering program at a 4-year university. "Taking care of yourself means taking control of your own life." I told her that I cared about what happened to her, and I really do. You have to start by showing you care, then they begin to care, too.

On Learning to Be Tough in the Inner City

I asked Jolie how she had built this strong conviction to redefine the work of schools as a hopeful, caring, and nurturing environment that moves youth to learn more about themselves and other peoples in the world. Her response was quick as she claimed there wasn't any "hard data" but that she could attribute some of her strength and integrity to family, African American and community role models, and neighborhood support for learning. All three she believes are partners in the learning process.

> My parents were working-class people. My grandparents came up from the South during the time of the Black migration, during the 20s, I think. Growing up in the South, my grandparents wanted their kids to do better. So, for at least several generations, there was a drive that "you got to do better!" My grandmother, I think had an eighth-grade education, my grandfather had a little lower. Both my parents have a high school education. In my neighborhood, I had role models. There were people of color who had gone on to college, who were teachers, lawyers, and professional people. They always had options but had to put up with a lot of things, like segregation and Jim Crow laws. I liked the fact that they were always in control of their lives. That is what motivated me, that I could have control of my life and I could achieve and accomplish anything.

Jolie understands how difficult it is for today's young, inner-city students to take risks in a world where everyone seems to have failed them. Given this, she works tirelessly in her capacity as school counselor. Jolie locates human resources, social services, and financial supports that provide the student and the student's family with the foundation needed for success. In addition, she often shares with students her own struggles against negative stereotypes, institutional barriers, and marginalization.

> My building is a very rough place. I was the first, for a lot of girls, Black, single, female professional they'd ever met that didn't have children. Most of the [students] assume that I have children. "You don't have kids?" They'd ask in astonishment. Remember, it's their experience that having kids at an early age is normal. "No," I say, "I'm going to wait until I'm finished with my education." Then, I share with them what I truly think and feel about having a family. There are times that this really makes a difference, and there are equally as many times I have to put my foot up their butts. I do have to say "NO!" I am the disciplinarian, the ogre, but, I tell the kids, "I'm here for you."

Jolie's commitment to learning stretches beyond the 8:00 a.m. to 3:30 p.m. school day. One evening a week, she conducts a special tutoring session for all eighth-grade students. She attends many of the students' evening and weekend activities and performances. She visits the homes of many of her students, and she writes a monthly newsletter to the parents, guardians, and families of all eighth-grade students. When Jolie gave me a tour of the middle school, I was impressed that she knew so much about the school's architectural structure and was fluent in the history of the school's personnel, curriculum, problems, and changing community context. Jolie believes that teachers and administrators must know the history of their schools and neighborhoods. "Knowing where we've been and who we need to stay connected with gives us power and know-how to make changes in our classrooms and schools that benefit the kids. Sounds simple doesn't it?" Walking through the halls, she pointed to specific places in the building, telling stories of what had occurred in "this spot" last month, last year, even 5 years before. She talked with students passing in the hall, addressing each by name and making sure she made eye contact and said something positive. She admitted that at times, it was difficult to say something positive, but she'd figure out something, "Even if it's to say they're clean behind the ears!" Whenever Jolie talked about the students, her voice became very clear, her gaze intense, and she would speak gracefully with her hands. She shares,

> The person who provides the opportunities for kids to learn also provides the nurturing and the discipline. Sometimes, it's the foot up the butt, but more often, it's the needed hugs. Whatever that child needs to encourage learning, we, the teachers and school counselors, are here to provide it. I loaned a child a dollar today. Now, my policy is, don't loan money, but . . . she got a dollar out of me. Jessica, I love her dearly, she didn't come to school at all last year. She is coming to school now. At first, we tolerated each other. Now, we like each other and we can sit down and talk. I said to a security officer at our school the other day, "If I was 13 or 14 again and I was going to walk the mean streets of my community and I needed someone to cover my back, I'd have Jessica. No one messes with Jessica." She is a lovely child who is trying to grow up with very little guidance. She wants to go to high school the second semester this year, but

she realized that she screwed up. She said, "I messed up, didn't I?" I said, "Yeah, Jessica, so you'll be with me all year." Now, she comes to school everyday, not necessarily on time, but I believe in baby steps. That was my first goal, to get Jessica back in school. The second goal is to help her learn.

Leadership Begins With Respect

Jolie's efforts as a summer school principal are grounded in her commitment to show students that adults do care and that everyone, regardless of age or situation, is due respect and justice. This was evident in her open and honest communication with the school staff.[2] She admits that her advocacy for teamwork, open discussions, shared decision making, and individual and collective responsibility to the "student first" was met with some uneasiness by secondary school teachers. Because she approached faculty with "respect and support structures that helped them do their job in the classroom," she was able to energize cooperation, trust, and dialogue among a faculty used to working in isolation. Through it all, she admits to learning to become a more effective, sensitive, and caring leader.

Each teacher comes to school with a different perspective of who I am and what they want me to do. I believe in working with and giving teachers feedback. There was this child who was taking trig[onometry], and his mother called to say that he was enjoying the class and doing all his homework. I later talked with his teacher, and I said, "I just got off the phone with Mrs. Y, and she was very happy and wanted me to share with you what a wonderful job you're doing with her son. He enjoys math. Thank you." I guess that teacher was surprised, because he said, "I've taught for 20 years and no administrator has ever thanked me for teaching." Another example of how I approach teachers in a nurturing way is through journal writing. This is helpful for the cadet [novice] teachers that I work with. During the first 2 weeks of school, I make sure I meet with each one. Their journals are valuable sources of information, real learning. Finally, I debrief myself every day. I ask myself, "What did I do? What could I do differently? What could I improve on? What were my successes and my mistakes? What didn't I do?" I wrote in my journal that my goals are to have fun, to smile more, and to learn.

Dealing With "Overt and Passive Racism"

Equity and justice in education is a powerful theme throughout Jolie's story. As we spoke more about the critical moments in her life (she liked to call them "learning adventures") that she believed help shape her work in schools, she talked about the empowerment and optimism that came from her own school experiences. She recalled a fourth-grade event that she thought helped her future educational successes.

> There was a point in my life, fourth grade, I took a test and was placed in a top reading group. At that time, our school was not integrated. I began to read books about the world, and I began to see the subtleties of the realities of life. I didn't call it racism or any other ism at the time—I was too young to label the issues—but just the way things were. I was interested in the things that we read and discussed. It was heavy stuff for kids.

Because of her own educational success, Jolie has little tolerance for people who "write off the kids" and behave in a "getting by" mode.

> The most difficult moment right now for me is having to deal with the overt and passive racism that exists in our public school system. I use to tell myself it didn't exist, it wasn't there. I don't believe that anymore because I'm now stepping outside of being defensive. I'm seeing it in ways where teachers will not teach the kids. You have "them" in your room, you walk into the room, you size it up, and you decide, "I'll ditto them to death!" I see it in situations where we don't take the time to learn that certain behaviors are not counterproductive but that there's a story there. If the school is truly to be a learning community, then yes, teachers and administrators need to understand the life situations of the students and their families.
> We need to get teachers, especially majority teachers, to get out of this "I feel so sorry for this child" rut. I talk about majority

[White] teachers because, in my experience, there are many that have stopped nurturing the "other" child. I throw in racism because if you listen to their talk, there's a sense that they've given up on the lower-income child, the child in the hood, "those" kids.

Jolie's statement that racism is embedded in schools began a deeper conversation focused on the boundaries, call them race or gender or both, that serve to exclude women of color from participating in educational leadership. It was revealing for us both, researcher and storyteller, that we spoke with clarity, certainty, and authority about leadership but still had to "address the comment— 'Oh, you're here because you're filling a quota.' "

Because of this, we have had to learn to speak with certainty, especially if you're going to be a leader. We have to confront head on those who doubt our intellectual capabilities because we're Black or Brown and women.

Interviewer: You speak very strongly about this.

Jolie: Because I know, I live it! I am living this and dealing with this every day! As a person of color, you're defined a certain way the moment you walk into any environment. For the longest time in my building, other teachers perceived I was a wealthy, upper-class Black woman. I have to chuckle because that wasn't my background at all. Another example is Miss Jones, I love her dearly. When I ask my eighth graders to name the teacher who has had the most impact on them, they either name an elementary school teacher or Miss Jones. The kids say it is because she helped them to learn how to write. She's African American, and she too isn't taken seriously. The other teachers say, "Well, that's Miss Jones. All the kids listen to her because she's African American." They don't take the time to see what she does for the kids. They can come up with 4,000 excuses instead of saying, "She's an exemplar teacher."

Jolie makes it clear that what she models daily is the philosophy that equity and choice come when a person is respectful of differences and responsible for self and community. "This attitude, this daily practice, is the responsibility of everyone who works with children!" She is convinced that without choices, which many of her young charges don't believe they have, both personal and cognitive growth cannot be realized. "Every individual," she added, "has the right to make decisions according to her [or his] own life script and not someone else's, and [know] that her [or his] choices will be valued and respected." Yet the themes of choice and equity that encourage students to grow in personal and cognitive ways and empower students to believe in themselves are often not a part of the larger school script. This school text is equally unsupportive of progressive teachers and school leaders who want to make a difference.

> In our schools, we still have people who adhere to the old paradigms. They just don't see a need to change. . . . I have a nice building administrator. He is a fun-loving individual, but his leadership is very, very weak. A lot of times, you go around asking, "Who's in charge?" After you get the answer, it's more or less a demoralizing feeling because you know that any of your ideas, anything you want for the school, will not get done. We were going to do peer mediation and peer counseling this year. The staff got all gung-ho about it. We had staff meetings and presentations back in October. This is now January, and we haven't done very much of anything. He's there, but we don't expect too much.

Jolie's story reveals her understanding of the rigid, mechanical organization of schools that often stands in the way of more progressive and caring work. If required, Jolie could spin the traditional yarns of appropriate roles and duties that the school elite would expect a veteran of 22 years to do. Yet her story also cries out in a resistant and forceful voice. She isn't joyful about surviving in an oppressive situation. During one such exchange, she grew very angry, frustrated with the ignorance that surrounded her.

> I have had teachers and administrators in my building who have said to me, "Good girl." I have had to stop and say, "No, you can call me a woman, you can say good job, but don't do the *girl* thing." It's taken me years to get that out of their minds. They don't see it as a problem. One of the counselors I work with re-

fers to the children as "those" kids. Her words were, "*Those* kids don't need arts and culture classes. Let's face it." This is divisive behavior!

The notes she hits are often trenchant, incisive, and sarcastic. She wasn't joyful about surviving in an oppressive situation, sharing an explosive confrontation that began with a teacher commenting:

> "*Those* kids don't need arts and culture classes. Let's face it."
> This is really divisive behavior! This is what I am working against! I want to feel that I am making a difference. I use to say to myself, I do not want to be a school administrator because it was hard work filled with many traps, and I love the quiet and the sanctity of my personal time. My motivation now is to be a school administrator. I want to learn and be involved with many different learning experiences. I know it will be hard, but the hardest things I've had to learn in my life was to drive a stick shift and put in contact lenses. The fact is, I did it. I know that no matter what challenge is thrown at me, I have the fortitude, the tenacity, the guts to do it.

Jolie has become a powerful and brilliant school leader committed to the best practices of teaching and learning, to "self" and "other" respect, and "to the joy and hope schools can offer." During our final conversation, Jolie confided,

> I hope someone will say that my presence did make a difference, and I hope it will be a positive difference. I want to say that I help kids, I help kids dream, and that I hope I help them reach their dreams.

Notes

1. I conducted my interviews with Jolie over a 1-year period. Since our interviews, we have maintained a close friendship. During the past 2 years, Jolie has become more involved in many school, community, and university activities. Jolie has recently accepted an assistant principalship position in New York.

2. My observation of Jolie's interpersonal relations with teachers, staff members, and parents revealed a strong sense of trust, which is absent in many teacher-administrator relationships. A teacher confided that she often disagreed with Jolie but that they always sat down and talked over their conflicts and "always worked it out to benefit the students. This is why I respect and trust Jolie."

7

The Golden Cord
That Speaks to My Soul

Opal's Story—
A Chinese American Woman

When you work you are a flute through whose heart the whispering of the hours turns to music, . . . And what is it to work with love? It is to weave the cloth with threads drawn from your heart, even as if your beloved were to wear that cloth.

—Kahlil Gibran (1923/1951), *The Prophet*

One of the many lessons my elders taught me was that a friend is a person who shares what is often hard to give—the gift of friendship is wisdom, reason, and compassion of the soul. As I read Opal's interview transcripts and journal writings, I realized she had given me the gift of her friendship. Without hesitation, she disclosed the keynotes, undertones, and overtones of the deepest parts of her soul. In her telling, she taught me about the need to be calm, to be at peace, so that the creative soul might work its miracles. The stories she told about her work in elementary schools and community service groups illuminated the love and compassion that drives her to make a difference in the lives of children.

On Being a Retired Teacher

Recently retired after 40 years of service in public education, Opal admits that retirement scared her: "Teaching and children had been integral to my life. What was I going to do? But it all worked out." Opal continues to work in the schools mentoring novice teachers, volunteering as a tutor, and developing programs for at-risk Black youth and multiage classes. Always a lifelong learner, Opal is active in a curricular movement that stresses whole-brain and kinesthetic learning. Her commitment to whole-brain and body learning comes as a result of her study and interest in natural ways of healing, such as reflexology. Because Opal is an avid reader, retirement has also meant that she now has time to digest volumes of work by philosophers, historians, and educators. Opal said of retirement, "It has given me time to reflect, to think about what I've done, and to plan what I want to do."

In this spirit of reflection, I asked Opal to share three artifacts that were metaphors for her work as an educator. Opal, in turn, defined my challenge as an opportunity for her to share what she called the dimensions of her soul. First, she introduced a slim silver bamboo bracelet, which she carefully removed from her wrist. She cautioned, "I rarely take this off but for you, . . . " Next, she held firmly a small egg carved from pine wood, which she squeezed softly and rolled gently across her palms. Last, she handed me a large harmonica that belonged to her husband, who had passed away several years earlier. These were the symbols that she felt expressed her commitment to children, to family, and to learning. She talked first about her silver bracelet:

> This silver bamboo bracelet is from Hong Kong. It is a complete circle. The significance of bamboo is its flexibility and strength; its ability to shift and sway yet still remain rooted. I always wear this, I never take it off.

Bamboo: The Union of
Inner Strength and Outward Flexibility

What Opal began to teach me that afternoon, sitting in her kitchen drinking hot black tea, was the symbolism of the bamboo. She explained that just as the earth depended on the rain to give life, the potential of one's work is dependent on the union of inner strength and outward flexibility. Opal expressed the need to understand that this union will meet many challenges, but we must be careful not to meet the challenges with fear or despair. She silently whispered, "You must be patient, strong, and flexible." Opal's family stories echoed this fundamental wisdom. She told of her oldest sister being held in prison during the Cultural Revolution in China and of her brother's perseverance against the debilitating effects of cerebral palsy. Opal also talked about her recent struggle to find inner peace after the death of her husband. "The principle that guides one's life," she pointed out, "is to be optimistic and maintain a heart of steadfastness and faith. This is deeply Chinese." After our interviews, she wrote in her journal, "Being optimistic is not being Pollyannish. It's a matter of choosing after seeing the positive points, the negative points, and the interesting points."

Being well rooted and flexible are qualities that seem to be born of the struggle of her parents, grandparents, and older sisters:

> My oldest sisters were left in China when my mother came to America. My grandfather was a very old-fashioned tyrant who desperately wanted grandsons, but my mother kept bearing daughters. So my dad, who was working in the U.S., went back to China in 1932 to bring my mom and the youngest of the children, Sally, back to America. They left the two older sisters, Ann and May, in China with family. When they got here, my mom gave birth to me in 1933, another daughter! I was followed by another girl child, Milly. When Milly was born, grandfather was livid. Fortunately, for mother's sake, Harry was born a year later, and then Jimmy followed. We had a good life, but it was a hard one, too. We had ended up in Zanesville, Ohio, about 54 miles away from a large Chinese settlement in Columbus, Ohio. This is where several of my relatives, my grandfather, and some friends had set up their laundry business. My father wasn't able to continue his education as he had to work in the family laundry business, although his younger brother, my uncle, was able to go to a large private university. Well, the intention was that my father and mother were going to make enough money to return to China. As it happened, my father's mother ended up raising my two older sisters. All our lives, we heard about these wonderful two older sisters. The oldest had spent 14 years in a prison camp because she was a physician. When Chairman Mao

died, she was released and given minimal back pay. Everyone had a confession on file about their supposed guilt; she wasn't guilty of doing anything, just being a physician. She was good at pretending to be brainwashed during those years of Communist rule. Both of my sisters are physicians.

Teaching in elementary schools for nearly 40 years, Opal believes that what she brought to the classroom was her commitment to encourage students to build their knowledge as well as develop their own pathways to inner strength. Opal believes that a vital quality of character one must develop is learning to be internally balanced: "You must be secure and comfortable with yourself so that you can be flexible and know that change is a natural ebb and flow." She added, "You don't get balance and then that's it. It's a process of always working to keep yourself in balance with yourself and with your environment." In the classroom, Opal worked to find a balance between her ways of teaching and the children's multiple learning styles. Over many years, she has experimented and employed many ways of teaching math, science, and reading. Her experiences have taught her that children learn best when they understand what they already know and are able to see what more they can know. Her own openness to learning has led her to incorporate multiple teaching tools. Opal integrates art, experiential learning, one-on-one instruction, student team learning, peer coaching, storytelling, discussion, and individual and group reflection processes. This variety, she believes, provides the students with many opportunities to learn and to take ownership in their own learning.

To explain this lesson of flexibility, letting go of long-held personal paradigms, Opal sketched a picture that illustrated the need to get rid of debris that clutters an upward and outward spiral path. As she drew, I began to understand that discarding ideas that are comfortable but not necessarily useful had been difficult for Opal. Then again, it would be difficult for anyone. Yet as she drew, there was a sense of fearlessness, of not being afraid to reach out and touch the "rawness" of the next moment in one's life. Opal had translated this personal insight to understanding the reasons students got stuck in one mathematical manipulation or on one reading level. The first step out of the rut, she said, was always overcoming self-doubt and fear of failure: "By the time they reach third and fourth grades, they have learned that it is not okay to make mistakes. Because they don't extend themselves, they get stuck."

To provide students with the skills to be flexible, to not be afraid to make mistakes while reaching for the next discovery, has become an underlying theme in Opal's teaching. Because she realized early on that children needed each other's support, she facilitated "class circle discussions" during which students talked about character issues, such as honesty, respect, and trust and learning processes, such as taking risks, collaboration, and letting go of ways of thinking and doing that no longer worked. This class conversation, coupled with many team activities, helped develop a community of learners in her classroom. Although some teachers saw Opal's class discussions and counseling as inappropriate and an obstacle to learning, over the years, Opal found that the group conversations enriched the learning experience for *all* students and "taught students to care and to share the responsibility of learning. This teaches not only individual respect but community commitment." The outcome may not have immediate results, such as students making the honor roll, but the life lesson Opal refers to is priceless.

Respect, trust, and honesty are lessons evident in many stories Opal shared about students she had worked with. One such story found a young African American student lumbering through his elementary school studies. Opal found that when she presented him with structured goals in a respectful manner, he began to respond. She often began by asking him to share what he had learned from family, friends, and the street. Listening respectfully and attentively, she would try to find something in his own life that she could connect to a math lesson or a reading assignment. Bit by bit, she increased the challenges in his work. Over time, he became more optimistic and self-assured, and his desire to learn and participate in class with other peers became more constructive. Although he may not have ended up a national scholar, he graduated from high school and is currently attending a 4-year college. "He's a winner!" Opal smiles broadly, "He could have fallen through the cracks and might have ended up in jail, but he learned to have faith in himself and respect the learning process."

Pinewood Egg: The Cycles of Life

The journey to find inner strength and a balanced life has led Opal and her students to many opportunities for new learning. To illustrate this point, she presented her second symbol, a small egg carved of pine wood:

> This egg carved from wood is something living. You can see the rings in the wood grain, which is a lifeline. I love the shape of it because it makes me think of new beginnings. I always have something to look forward to—to new cycles. Our lives are filled with endings and beginnings, much like this wooden carved egg. Each layer just makes the wood carving stronger, much like each new discovery makes our lives stronger. I like the way this egg feels; it is very tactile, much like our lives—we should be able to feel it. Children need to feel their lives, too. They need to know that the cycles of their lives create this egg. Knowing this, being able to understand and touch this idea, holds much promise.

The importance of the wooden egg metaphor strikes a deep chord in Opal's soul as it reminds her that the carving of her own life is deeply touched by the lives of others; and in much the same way, her life touches the lives of others in significant ways. Believing this required that she open her heart and genuinely respect and love her students. Opal admits that she probably never knew how important this lesson was until a young student, Ann Catherine Flowers, touched her life:

> When Ann Catherine Flowers was in my class as a 7 year old, she taught me so much by being so caring of others and so gentle. She was in an accelerated first- and second-grade combination. I had never taught such a potent class. Those kids could read and think so well that it was sometimes hard for me to keep up with them. They were so challenging. There was one little boy who was very naughty but excelled in math. Ann Catherine did not do well in math; in fact, she always got a stomachache during math. Now, even though this little naughty boy was not a favorite partner for the other children in class, Ann Catherine had a calming effect on him. She had the wisdom, at a very young age, to be kind to him. You know, just the way she looked at him, she was wonderful. She also had a lovely sense of humor, which often calmed the class and me, too. The following summer, Ann Catherine was killed while riding a horse. This

stopped me in my tracks because I had never known such a young death up close. Ann Catherine became a symbol to me and the children. She taught us that every child, even the naughty little boy, is special. All we needed to do was look beyond our own stereotypes and see the goodness in others. I don't know that I had been aware of the specialness of every child in such an unconditional way before. I do know that because her little life touched me, I became committed to recognize the uniqueness of every child and to create learning opportunities every day that gave every child a chance to shine. Ann Catherine's spirit is so alive in me!

Opal talked about the significance of the wooden egg: "It reveals that I have lost and won some battles, and I have many more ahead, but each is a layer that makes me wiser and makes my convictions stronger." It is her mission to assure young children that they will not lose their uniqueness and their heritage but, instead, that education can increase their understanding of who they are, perhaps what their own missions in life are, and it can help them come to know and respect their diverse global community.

"I Understood I Was a Chinese American Kid"

She explained that many of her own growing-up and school experiences reinforced the idea that she must cherish her uniqueness as a Chinese American woman as well as know the ways of others. Growing up in Zanesville, Ohio, where there were only three other Chinese families at the time, might have presented some difficulties. However, Opal admits that because her parents taught all the children the importance of respect and to look only at the "good in others' hearts," she never encountered problems. Opal shared her many visits to the flats, which was an African American community. Many of her parents' laundry employee families lived in the flats, where Opal has many memories of "good food, great music, and lots of dancing." She was also welcome at the tracks, the lower socioeconomic White neighborhoods, where many of her school friends lived. Her family often went into town to the movies and to restaurants, and on several occasions, she visited the terraces, a predominantly affluent White neighborhood. She explained that her family lived between the flats, town, and tracks: "We were different, didn't fit with the other groups, but I never felt that people thought badly about me personally." Opal doesn't deny that there were class and racial tensions in the community; in fact, during the war years, because she was of Asian ancestry, she began to feel the heat of her difference:

> I understood I was a Chinese American kid. We were often asked during the war years, "Are you Chinese or Japanese?" It must have been just terrible for a kid who was Japanese. What made me angry was that my best friend was German, but I didn't think she was a Nazi. I mean, her grandmother didn't speak any English, only German, but other kids and adults never asked her if she was a Nazi! It made me angry, do you know what I mean? Overall, I grew up in a good community where my parents were treated fairly and with respect and my brothers and sisters were always treated very nicely.

Some of Opal's Asian women friends, who were sent to Japanese detention camps or were in cities that often oppressed Asian families, believe that Opal and her family were "mascots" for their predominantly White community. Her friends argue "that just being kind to a Chinese family doesn't mean that you're not racist." One friend even suggested that as long as Opal's family

> did laundry and did not live in the terraces, the family members would always be treated neighborly. But if they had overstepped their role in the community or if one of the children became a troublemaker, the family would have been treated differently.

Opal responded thoughtfully to these statements:

> Some women resent my story and say I am a Chinese mascot. I don't think so because someone who is being treated like a token anything is a kind of toy that does what everyone else wants her to do. I felt respect. I didn't feel a lot of pressure to behave a certain way or to stay in certain places. My brothers and sisters and I traveled all over our community and were never spoken rudely to. We were very lucky, we had wonderful experiences.

We worked hard, we were respectful of others, and we got a lot of recognition from our community.

Despite her unique situation, Opal understands the sadness and the anger of other Asian women who have been devalued by the communities in which they have lived. In fact, she admits that her daughter often feels the tension of marginalization, but Opal continues to teach benevolence and self-respect as the keys to overcoming the frustration of alienation:

> My daughter, who was in high school at the time, and I were in an elevator at a ski resort. Another passenger in the elevator asked us, "What country are you from?" My daughter was pretty insulted; she stared at him in disbelief and retorted, "We're from Michigan!" Her face showed her inner thoughts of, "What planet are you from!" We got off the elevator at the next floor, even though it wasn't our floor. I tried to calm her down. She thought that the man was so stupid. I tried to explain to her that he probably had limited experience with Asian people and that if she listened to his voice, he was trying to be friendly. She couldn't see it. I know I have to key into where my daughter is coming from. I suppose I don't jump to judgment as quickly, and I've learned that it takes too much negative energy to prove yourself instead of just being yourself. I understand the resentment, it's just so much wasted energy.

On "Getting Beyond the Squabbling"

It might appear that Opal is accommodating and accepting of ignorance. I questioned her extensively about her thoughts toward racism. She never talked about how she might have been discriminated against but told only stories about how she recognized others being marginalized. She has no patience with any activity that segregates children or excludes important information from learning experiences. In fact, she channeled her energy in a proactive manner when she found that history lessons taught in K-12 schools in her state excluded the experiences of Japanese Americans during World War II. Deeply rooted in her belief in justice and equity, Opal helped to form a group of Asian Pacific women whose purpose was to press the schools and policy-making boards to change what was being taught. She shared,

> It was pretty political because we wanted to get involved in a way that would allow us to have some power in the legislature. We then moved our work into the schools because we felt as teachers, we could make an impact. We met with many people trying to find a way to impact the curriculum in terms of adding more information. We educated ourselves about the experiences of Chinese Americans, Japanese Americans, and others in the United States. You rarely hear these views in schools. You hardly even get to explore all the dimensions of World War II. There's a lot about Black history, and not that you don't want to omit any of it, but there's very little about the Asian experience here. Here's the thing, because my children never learned about the Asian view in schools, they didn't think it was important.

There is, Opal admits, much tension between people with different beliefs, but she thoughtfully says, "If we care about our society at all, we have to go beyond that." Here, the significance of Opal's first symbol, the bamboo bracelet, can be applied. Bamboo shafts were often balanced across one's shoulder to carry heavy loads tied or hung on them. This flexibility and strength keeps Opal mindful of her personal commitment to "get beyond the squabbling" and to build bridges "between different people, different ideas, and different groups wherever and whenever I can. Sometimes, I feel like I'm a bridge in a no-man's land, but I work hard to link people together." I point out that carrying this weight can be cumbersome, to which Opal quickly responded,

> I learned that the llama is an animal that will simply sit down when they can no longer carry its load. That sensibility of knowing enough is enough is the balance I often look for. What a great symbol of wisdom!

Harmonica: "Teaching and Leading Is Like Jazz Music"

Mentioning that Opal's egg and bamboo bracelet have certainly strengthened her advocacy for all children, she replied:

At times, I'll say, I'm a feminist. In the past, White feminism did not fit my thinking, but ethnic women, especially African American women, have joined the movement. I believe that Asian women and indigenous women must also join that dialogue and be advocates for a variety of issues. I fight for children and family rights. When I define myself as a feminist, I'm relating to women and men who are spiritually strong. They are people who have stopped the complaining and are making a difference. The voice I use is one that is speaking for those who haven't had the opportunity but are strong, dedicated, intelligent, caring women.

Opal's final symbol, a harmonica that she gave to her husband, describes her teaching, school leadership, and passion for the arts. She said of this gift,

I want to play this harmonica. It's my husband's (long pause)— it's got great tones. I gave it to him when we were first married, let's see, in 1957. It was one of our first gifts. He was very good at it. I haven't learned to play it, but I picked it up because it reminds me of living; that is, life is like music. School is like an orchestration. Teaching has to have music, not just the melody but all the dynamics that set the mood. Children are looking, waiting, to hear the beat. I have to breathe to get the tones I want from the harmonica. The tensions in schools occur because we don't breathe, we don't pause to observe our rigid movements, and so we don't shift to more rhythmic, flowing movements. Music, like teaching, requires discipline but also the freedom to be creative. Music, like learning, is universal and holistic.

Opal would say, "teaching and leading is like jazz music." The more I thought on this, the more the metaphor made sense to me. A jazz musician combines notes and tones, color and tempo, and chords and movements in multiple variations. Teaching and leading also require the use of many tools, in different combinations, to build learning environments and develop ways of learning that are creative and child centered. For example, school buildings and school classrooms haven't changed much in Opal's 40-year career; she says, "The classrooms are still boxes and we [teachers] have to work hard to make them look like fun places to be." Instead of square buildings, sharp corners, rows of desks, and sterile walls and linoleum floors, Opal suggests additions of color, recessed lighting, round tables, windows; "graceful curves, natural wood, soothing color tones, and living plants can make a learning environment an inviting place." She continued:

> It's a myth to think that all children who come to school in kindergarten are ready. Or that by the third or fourth grade, they are all at the same level. Yet we somehow keep making decisions about how our buildings should look, how we ought to set up our classrooms, and how and what we must teach, as if there were no differences. We need to build time into our school schedule for each precious child to develop their knowledge and their self-esteem in schools that are designed for optimal learning. The way schools are designed, the way they have always been designed, is scary!

Although Opal has seen many classrooms that are child centered—with exploration centers, spaces for individual or student-directed study as well as large group or teacher-directed work, introduction of technology, use of the visual and media arts, tables arranged in half moons and circles or clusters, plants and plant experiments, fish tanks, carpet and pillow corners for reading, and so on—she still finds many classrooms that are stark, with rows of desks facing the chalkboard. As a mentor to young teachers, Opal shares her vision of how classrooms might be arranged: "As a setting that says 'come on in, let's learn together and make things happen!' The important thing is to focus on the children first!"

Another dimension of Opal's vision of the school environment is focused on the family. Again, her symbol of the harmonica plays softly beneath her thoughts as she explains that children learn for the entire family. Opal and her siblings attended public K-12 schools and all went on to a college or university. Although her parents never demanded that they do well nor offered the children bribes for high grades, Opal said, "All of us knew that education was important because education was something no one could take from us." Because Opal's father and mother had never finished their formal schooling and both were not as fluent in English as the children, Opal and her brothers and sisters often shared their school lessons with their parents. This was not a responsibility that Opal or her siblings took lightly. Because of this experience, she believes that children today are learning new things every day that must be shared with their families. The idea that the child learns for the family suggests that the student takes home what she or he is learning, and the family must build on this in experiential ways:

> Parents or guardians are very important to a child's success in school. I really honor the fact that parents have certain values and desires for their children. I say to parents, "Look, this educational experience is very important to you and to your child, so I want to know what you want for your child." I ask them because then I can explain what I'm doing, and together we can get on the same alignment. We work together.

Educating the family also means providing students with experiences that broaden their vision of the global world. As a strong supporter of multicultural education, Opal has worked with many school leaders to define and implement programs that introduce other cultures in meaningful ways. For example, working with her former school principal, Opal was able to help institute a student trip abroad to visit an elementary school in Taiwan. A group of Taiwanese students studying at the nearby university prepared and presented 16 lessons, focused on Taiwanese lifestyles and history, for the children in grades four and five. Later that school year, Opal, several teachers, a counselor, an administrator, parents, and a group of fourth- and fifth-grade children visited Taiwan.

I asked Opal why she never became a building-level principal. She explained that the gift of leadership was not bound in a role but in actions that benefit children. Opal has always seen herself as a leader, although she may not have taken on the "position" of leader. She also defined leadership as a team effort. In college, she held a student leadership position in which she worked with other inspiring young adults on school reform efforts and community service projects. She had learned that sharing the function of leadership did not diminish individual and collective commitment but strengthened their ability to attain their goals. Of course, she admits, there were disagreements, but because they had built a trusting relationship and were clear on their purpose, the tensions often helped them to think more clearly and get the work done more successfully. These early lessons have pressed Opal to develop teaming opportunities among teachers in her schools.

> After 40 years of teaching, I can look back and say that I have always worked for and with men and women who were excellent teachers. I was always a part of dynamic discussions among teachers and principals. We would always ask, "How will this benefit the children?" or "How will we make this a win-win situation in the lives of children, teachers, and families?" I have always worked with teams of teachers because networks are strong resources that help us to be bridges for our students.

How did her metaphors, the bamboo bracelet, wooden egg, and harmonica, help Opal to define a vision for schools? She replied to my query with passion:

> The vision of schools must be attached to the human spirit. We must find ways to free our institutions in order to unlock possibility. This is the creativity that allows the human spirit to soar. To me, the elements of arts and the humanities integrated with academics is a way. Also, I believe that teachers must be leaders. They must be given the authority and power to make choices and to define the mission of a school with the needs and well-being of children clearly in focus. Right now, schools tend to bend to the louder voices that never have the good of all children in mind, only the good of the elite.

For Opal, her strength has come from a lifelong journey of coming to knowing her soul and the world she lives in. This dynamic interaction has helped her to transcend the material and finite pieces of her existence and to attend to and share a spirit that honors deep reflection, breadth of vision, and giving abundantly. Her intention is genuine; her caring and love are precious gifts. My father taught me that the company one keeps is a reflection on one's own quality of character. I have been in good company, and I believe that every child that has walked with Opal has had a companion who has given what is often difficult to give, a soul that supports, advises, protects, sacrifices, and rejoices.

8

I Come From Gray

Rachel's Story—
A Japanese American Woman

Nothing so gentle, so adaptable, as water, yet it can wear away that which is hardest and strongest.

—Lao-tsu

"I come from gray," says Rachel Yukimura, a Japanese American Buddhist who resists the impetus of schools to control, to label, to fix things in black-and-white terms. As the vice principal of a suburban elementary school, she struggles to remain open in a world that pushes her to make judgments. In many ways, her life is lived in opposition to the tenets of public schooling, and yet this opposition is as quiet and gentle as water flowing over a rock.

This image, in fact, is one she uses to describe her father. He was "like rock and water." He was like rock, Rachel says, because of his strong set of values. He gave her a philosophical foundation, a sense of "how you live a life." Yet he was like water, a deep thinker and fluid, able to talk about his feelings in a way most men of his generation could not. Today, Rachel echoes her father's life, as she, too, becomes like water flowing over, around, and against the world of public education in Hawaii.

About Schools

Rachel describes her current school of 660 students as an anomaly among the schools in her district. Most of the district is filled with lower socioeconomic homes, people on welfare, unemployment, poverty and its attendant problems. Her present school is primarily middle class, with a very stable teaching staff and few real discipline problems. The surrounding community is made up of military families, mainland transplants, and locals in about equal proportions.

The school is changing, beginning to face a few problems, such as overcrowding and the creep of poverty into the community. This past year, the school sacrificed its library to create two more classrooms because of overcrowding. The school grounds are dotted with portables that have been there for years, set down one by one as the school grew. It presently has 13 permanent classrooms and 14 portables. The school also now serves free or reduced lunches to more than one quarter of the children, a number that has mushroomed in the past few years. Still, in comparison to its sister schools, it is in good shape. All the children leave Rachel's current school literate, and test scores are at or around the national norms.

These children, however, who are relatively free of problems, are not the children Rachel is drawn to. It is the poorer children farther out on the coast that call to her. The children whose test scores she describes as "dismal" (the lowest in the state) and who remain shockingly illiterate through all of their elementary years are the ones that draw her interest. She says she feels more at home out there, partly because of her plantation background and partly because she loves a challenge. "Boring!" she says, "Working in a middle-class school with few discipline problems is sometimes boring." Beyond this, Rachel is unable to really articulate what draws her to the poor coastal communities of Hawaii. In the end, she says simply that it is "a place that I feel drawn to."

Despite the poverty, these communities contain "wonderful Hawaiian children," Rachel recalls, like Walter, who could not read or write but could draw beautifully. He exhibited a different way of knowing and learning, illustrating his understanding of nerves, muscles, and anatomy through his drawing of a frog in science class. "We have much to learn from these children," Rachel insists. "They teach us about other ways of knowing, about multiple intelligences. They help us to reconsider what and how we teach."

In these coastal areas the "needs reach so deep into the community in so many ways." One solution Rachel sees is to develop the school as a community service center. At the present time, education is but one of many "disparate, linear, separated services in the community." Instead, the school needs to become a lifelong learning center, where the many efforts of agencies are integrated and a community of learners is built.

This sense of community echoes Rachel's early life on the plantation, where she felt "connected to everybody . . . the man with the piggery, the kerosene man," everyone in the community. Her parents ran a general store, and they lived in the back of the store, so all the members of the community moved in and out of their lives almost daily. In that small community, "Everybody was to be cared for," Rachel says, "We were all human, all special. The community was one." Everybody had a station, but "all were valued as members of the community." Thus, when Rachel was working on the coast, she felt that same sense of community. "I felt connected to the students, the parents, the cafeteria workers, the teachers," she says.

The Positive Anomaly

Rachel's own sense of being different began when she drew a map of her neighborhood for a geography class in college. She drew the one paved road down the middle of the plantation, lined by big white houses, and then the red cinder roads that led to her father's store, the Japanese camp, the Buddhist Temple, the Filipino Camp, the Hawaiian Camp, and so on. Suddenly, gazing at that map, the fact of her difference hit her full force. Before that, her world had felt safe, seamless, a paradox of separations that felt whole. Growing up in Hawaii was "very healthy." No one thought of these groups as separated by ethnicity or religion. Even though the center of her existence was Japanese school and the Buddhist Temple, "When we graduated from high school," she reports, "we all went to every baccalaureate in town."

While Rachel's husband was in graduate school, they lived in a trailer park in Illinois. One day her neighbor, Alberta, was complaining about "all those Black people." When Rachel replied, "Alberta! What are you saying? Look at me!!" Alberta said, "Oh, you don't count. You're invisible." "That was really amazing to me," recalls Rachel.

> It really struck me, in terms of how people see me or Asian people. . . . Then, I began to think about what it meant to be a minority, because when you grew up in Hawaii, you grew up with a "majority" attitude.

Rachel describes herself as a "positive anomaly." Responses to her from people in the Midwest, where she went to college, were mostly positive. She came to the Midwest, she says, "with no baggage."

"I really learned about what it meant to be Japanese American when we lived in Seattle," says Rachel. She describes Hawaii as

> strangely, wonderfully, sometimes sadly insulated. . . . My life hasn't been full of a sense of being a minority at all, but now that I look back, I think there's a strand of that that's come through since I've left Hawaii.

With thousands of Asians in Seattle, she became part of "an identifiable minority within the community." Rachel told the story of her son's first day of kindergarten in Bellevue, Washington. He was almost the "only Asian kid in the school" and when he came home on the bus, he went to stand in front of the mirror, pulling at the corners of his eyes and asking, "Mom, what's a Chinaman?" Rachel answered, "That's someone who is from China, why?" Other children on the bus had been teasing him. "That's part of the reason we've come home," Rachel says, "for our children to have had the opportunity to grow up, as I did, with a 'majority' sense, rather than a minority stance."

Being Tiny in the Universe

Rachel prefers to see herself as a very small part of an infinitesimal universe rather than a large part of the very small world of education in Hawaii. She talked about having a "life sense" rather than a "career sense," an "inside sense of who I am and how tiny I am in the universe." She likes the idea of being insignificant in the natural world because it gives her a sense of humility, a sense that she really is like everyone else, the same fears and joys as the school custodian or a parent. It also adds to her sense of wonder at the vast world we live in.

What attracted her, made her laugh and laugh, was the image of herself as a leader on a tricycle, no white horse, no Cadillac, or train, but furiously riding her 10" wheels across the playground to the edge of the schoolyard each day and then dragging it back to her office to start out again the next day. A tricycle, for her, seems to add the sense of humility and laughter she needs to symbolize the daily realities of her work. She believes that each of us needs to laugh at ourselves, to stand back and look at what it is we all do, how seriously we take ourselves, and to sense that our struggles, in the context of our vast universe, are very "trikelike."

Rachel discussed her existence as a woman in the very male world of educational administration. She says she is not a feminist; "I don't like labels," she states firmly. Recently, on a trip with her daughter to Washington, D.C., her daughter asked her, "Mom, how can you say you're not a feminist, given what you believe and how you live your life?" Rachel admitted that her values might be feminist, but she resists labels of all kinds: "They cast into hardened forms—affect the flow of life." She spoke of seeing the Holocaust Museum recently in Washington, D.C., the ways in which it brought home the destructiveness of labels.

Yet she is aware of the struggles and the inequality women have had to suffer and is most aware of gender as a factor in the work she does. Her sense of equity stretches beyond gender to class, race, ethnicity, embracing the illiterate, the poor, working always toward a sense of inclusion and community. She believes that women in Hawaii are creating a different kind of leadership, one she describes as "more open, more considerate of different ways, more inclusive." She discussed Gilligan's work on gender and the fact that Kohlberg's research on moral development had no scale for compassion and nurturing.

Clearly, Rachel uses both in her work, compassion for all the tiny creatures of the universe and nurturing for their growth and learning. She rejects the term feminist, first, because it is a label and she sees labels as divisive and stereotyping, but second, because the connotation of feminist for Rachel is someone who is an activist, who raises a fist with an armband on, the exact opposite of the way she works.

Multiple Realities

A black 150-pound wild pig once showed up in Rachel's backyard in suburban Hawaii. The whole family rushed to the kitchen window to see it. "Everybody had a different response to this same pig," Rachel reports. As they watched the pig root around in the bushes, her daughter, who loves animals, saw a young piglet, and said, "Can we keep the pig as a pet?" Her son, who was looking at the pig's tusks, saw danger, and said, "How do we get rid of it?" "Those pigs urinate in the streams," responded her husband, who used to work for the department of health. "That pig is nothing but a dangerous health risk, a bundle of leptospirosis." Rachel called her sister and told her about the pig, and her sister said, "There must be something spiritual about your house," because the pig is a family icon for many families in Hawaii. When she told her brother about the pig, his response was, "When's the luau?"

"Here is the reality," says Rachel, "there is a 150-pound black pig in our yard, and it's the first time it's come . . . yet everybody had a different take on this bunch of protoplasm."

> I reflected on that . . . what was the truth here? And I really came to see that that was essentially the reality for each person . . . everybody has a different perspective on the same thing—his or her own truth.

When Rachel moves into a new school, she says,

> Immediately, I would have people coming to me with questions, complaints, sometimes ideas . . . and there are times when I feel just from what I know, given an incident, that I would listen to one person, but I always try to make myself stay open and listen to both sides and not judge or pigeonhole. Because sometimes what is obvious is not "it."

She tries always to keep in mind that "people have separate realities." "I try to remain flexible," Rachel says, keeping an open mind and heart . . . when you're working with a group of people . . . adults in particular, because I think many of us as adults have come to trying to define what's right and wrong, what's good and bad, what's me versus you, them versus us, that kind of thing. Things sort of naturally work toward [dichotomies], and people say things like, "Take a stand! Which side are you on?"

But, says Rachel, "I come from gray." It is the bureaucratic view of the world, where things are often seen as black and white, that Rachel sees as dogmatic and often counterproductive. So she tries to remain open to the multiple realities of all who work in her school: the custodian, the school secretary, the teachers, the principal, and, of course, the children. Staying open to multiple interpretations means she often finds herself "wallowing in really messy stuff." Yet this enables her to stay open and to let things emerge, allowing for more creativity in solving the problems of public schools. Rachel describes this view as one of nonattachment, of opening your palm to things happening.

Education so often is driven by the need to control, to control children, budgets, and programs. By letting go, Rachel believes she is better able to let things grow, to be nurturing but not controlling, to allow growth and creativity. This "sense of living gray" is deeply rooted in her Buddhist background and the values she learned from growing up in the Japanese camp of the sugar plantation.

9

Remaking Childhood

Sarah's Story—A European American Woman Making Alternative Choices

> *That's what I mean to tell you. On the other side of the place you live stands a dark woman. She has been trying to talk to you for years. You have called the same name in the middle of a nightmare, from the center of miracles. She is beautiful. This is your hatred back. She loves you.*

> —Joy Harjo (1990, p. 38)

Sarah, an elementary school principal, describes herself as ordinary, a woman who often comes to school in slacks and a sweater that she has knitted in her rare spare moments. Her shoes are always flat so that she can move quickly and easily. Her makeup is simple, but she indulges herself in a hair color to lighten up her gray. Even though she is nearing 60, her figure is still slim and almost birdlike. Sarah looks like someone's sweet grandmother. "I don't look dangerous," she says, "but I am," and she smiles a quiet, knowing smile at me. Sarah's present school, Greene Elementary, is in one of the poorest parts of the city. On my way to her school, I pass an adult video store, a nude-dancing bar, and the Tidee Didee Diaper Service and Infant Furniture Store. The school sits next to a park, reclaimed by the children on weekdays from the drug users who own it nights and week-ends and who strew candy and cigarette wrappers along with used needles across the expanse of grass and dirt. The school children use it for their nature walks, science projects, and games.

After I greet Sarah in her office, she begins to introduce me to her staff as they drift into school the morning I am visiting. A woman with curly, damp hair, in a loose-fitting black and white checked shirt and trousers, comes over to the counter where we are standing. Sarah introduces her as Jane, the school's child development special-ist. Sarah says, "Some people say we are joined at the hip." Jane be-gins to ask Sarah about a grant proposal she is writing: "Do you want to see what I've written (for the narrative portion), or shall I just go ahead and turn it in?" "Would I make any changes?," asks Sarah. "What a crazy question!" I think, "How would Jane know whether Sarah would like what she wrote?" Then I realize that is exactly the point. Sarah trusts Jane to know her well enough to be able to tell whether she would make changes or not.

While Sarah talks to the other teachers as they arrive for the day, I become engrossed in a conversation with Charlotte, the elementary-grade-level chair who tells me how much she likes working at Greene Elementary. She says she lives way across town and could teach much closer to home, but the sense of community in the school keeps her there. The teachers socialize together outside of school, and this sense of caring and support are important to her.

Sarah calls me out into the hall, saying, "Joanne, you've got to see this!" She has a delighted smile on her face, and I wonder what she is so thrilled about. She leads me into the cafeteria where hun-dreds of children are gathered at tables finishing their breakfast. Kids run up to Sarah, hugging her around the knees and telling her hello, hungry for the contact. One frail little girl fingers her brown-streaked agate necklace and says it looks like a desert. Meanwhile, a large African American woman with a microphone at the other end of the cafeteria is dismissing the children to their classrooms, one table at a time. Outside the cafeteria, all the teachers stand at their classroom doors, greeting the children as they file into their rooms. The school day begins.

Once school begins, Sarah and I travel the halls, popping into open classroom doors to say hello, stopping to learn about special programs Sarah has created. One room is full of couches with an adult reading to a child or two on each couch. There are moms in jeans and sweatshirts, businessmen in suits, and grandmas and grandpas who have all come to tutor children in reading.

Down the hall is the Family Room, run by a full-time social worker who also has a background in education and early childhood development. Sarah introduces me to Marj, the director of the program, and to Kelly, a parent who is writing a poem at a computer in the room. Kelly is wearing a black T-shirt with "The Storm" on it and black tights with a hole in the knee. She is missing a front tooth and has a tattoo on her hand. She tells me that she is the mother of two boys and that Greene Elementary is "the best around." Kelly's oldest son has a learning disability, and she says he was sent home from one of the other schools he had attended because he couldn't learn. Now, because of Greene Elementary, Kelly announces proudly that her son is earning a B average in school.

The Family Program is composed of several parent groups who meet weekly and was started in 1994 with a block grant. Founded on the belief that parents are their children's first teachers, this program was initially designed to promote family literacy through the telling and writing of family stories. As the program progressed, so did the enthusiasm and commitment of the women involved. Through the Family Program, the women were also able to form friendships and become more actively involved within Greene Elementary and the community. They have been to the state legislature to lobby for educational causes and have successfully picketed a neighborhood tavern that wanted to expand its liquor license. The program is dedicated to reinforcing a positive sense of self and community by giving these parents a chance to share their stories with each other while simultaneously learning to reinscribe their own lives in ways that heal and bond. This program is founded on the work of Robert Coles (1989), author of *The Call of Stories: Teaching and the Moral Imagination* and Belenky, Clinchy, Goldberger, and Tarule's (1986) work on *Women's Ways of Knowing*, which underscores the importance of hearing, valuing, and strengthening the voices and stories of women.

This program, which is essentially Sarah's brainchild, is but one way her work as principal enriches the lives of children and parents at Greene Elementary. Sarah's convictions about education grow out of her belief in the power of language and out of her own history as an abused child. These conditions have given her the power to find her own way. "We've been a band of outliers," Sarah explains, "and we're in a school that used to . . . " Here she hesitates, because the school has been transformed under her leadership from one that no one wanted to be in to one that has a national reputation for excellence.

This journey has not been an easy one for Sarah. At one time, she was in so much trouble with the school district that she was banished to Greene Elementary, a place where no one wanted to go because of the impoverished environment. It was the district's dumping ground for "screw-ups." Sarah was a screw-up because of an open controversy at her old school over the use of whole language.

Five teachers followed Sarah from her previous school and began to work with the teachers at Greene, building a strong cadre of dedicated staff members. The other teachers at Greene "recognized right away how good they were and figured that if they were willing to come to such a hard school to work with me, I must be OK." Gradually, then, a close community of teachers began to form. "There began to be some momentum around that," Sarah believes. Here she credits the other teachers rather than just her own efforts: "I feel like I had an awful lot of help. . . . I didn't do it by myself."

Sarah believes that teachers must first be primarily caregivers and nurturers and that classrooms should be communities, safe places in which children can "risk learning." Seeing the fragile attachments Greene Elementary students had to their parents and other adults, Sarah reorganized the school "to bond teachers and kids for years." At the time, there was plenty of theory but no research on multi-grade-level classrooms. Sarah just felt intuitively that these children needed to be with the same teacher for several years, and so she created classrooms where children could stay across grades and grow in their sense of safety and attachment to their teachers.

"What schooling is not about," says Sarah, "is standards and benchmarks." She continues,

I'm furious with that whole political movement. The standards and benchmarks movement is a form of tyranny. It brutalizes kids, teachers, and educators in general by telling them that they "must do this or . . . " and the "or" is always left ambiguous and therefore even more frightening. . . . What we should be talking about (but we're not) is motivation. How can a learner be truly motivated? If the learner is motivated, that learner will exceed beyond any standards that anybody can dream up.

Sarah goes on to discuss the basic building blocks of motivation: "At the base of it, motivation is about not being hungry or sick or tired so that you're available to engage with learning." Yet this is precisely the condition in which many of Greene Elementary's children come to school.

"What I think we have here is a society that is not caring for its children. . . . In this society, I believe that doing well in school is a metaphor for children being well cared for." Thus, the standards and benchmarks movement comes into play when society tries to justify that it is caring for children. "If we can say a child has met these standards, what we're saying is we, as a society, have met our obligation to this child." This kind of thinking, Sarah believes, lets us off the hook as a nation, so we push schools and teachers to meet the standards we set in order to absolve ourselves of our responsibilities to children. "I really, really want to counter this whole standards thing," Sarah says. "I think it's insidious. I think it's perverse. I think it's terribly punishing . . . (and) it's not getting at the real questions about why children don't learn."

On Leadership

Sarah describes herself as a "nontraditional leader," one who has never fallen into line easily. She illustrates this point with a story about a personality test she took in college in the 1950s. The psychology major who gave the test came back and said her test had been invalidated because she answered specific questions incorrectly, such as whether you would rather walk across campus with the student body president or any regular student. Sarah remembers choosing any regular student because she "didn't care about walking with the student body president" and "didn't particularly like him." Sarah believes that bureaucracies are built on the notion that you want more than anything to please the person who is in power, and she states, "That has never been an issue for me." She feels her own difficult relationship with her father has contributed to this belief. Although he was the pillar of their small community when she was growing up, he was abusive, convincing her that authority figures are not always to be revered or even trusted. Given this, Sarah has not hesitated to disagree with the superintendent of schools, at first through confrontation and now by working through the system and using her support base: teachers and families.

Recalling her childhood, Sarah states that "I was always kind of a leader." As a kid, when neighborhood children would play school, she would be the teacher. "I was naturally bossy," she jokes. Originally, in her role as principal, Sarah feels she was not a very good leader. She describes herself as stiff, formal, and insincere. "I bought into the clear mission and goals stuff" and tried to "whip my staff on to excellence. . . . I think I did that pretty badly," she states. "I had to learn from the pain of a lot of my failures."

Today, Sarah feels she's changed, partly through her own growth as a person. "You're no better a principal than you are a person," she explains. Although she acknowledges that seeing yourself as a leader can be "pretty frightening" because "it creates an enormous sense of responsibility," she talks today about her leadership as being "organic," a sense of "paying attention to where life and interests are" and being a catalyst for the teachers in her school. Sarah says the word is out now, so that "innovative, pretty radicalized teachers want to come and work with me." Sarah values the work these teachers do. "I need them," she maintains. "They can do things that I can't do. They make a difference. Who they are and what the school has accomplished hasn't been what I've done so much as what they've done."

Sarah talked of being their spokesperson: "One thing I've been able to do is put words to who they are and to what they do, and I think they've come to appreciate and want that from me. They love being reflected in my words." This year, when Sarah conducted teacher evaluations, she found a way to use her own words to describe the work of teachers in her school. "For years and years and years and years, I've struggled with this nasty bureaucratic form that gives you little boxes to describe everybody's work in. And you can only respond to the same dreary questions, so I just threw it out," explains Sarah. "Instead, what I did was write a narrative description of our work together over the 2-year period, and it was just wonderful to read that with them. It was so much more, to have my real words coming back to them."

Sarah's values come through strong and clear in this statement, her belief in the power of narrative and her need for things to be real.

This need follows through in her personal relationships with teachers, too. "One of the things I've really learned over time and it was very, very hard," states Sarah, "is to be trusting enough to be transparent. We're friends, I mean really friends," Sarah states, speaking of her relationships with the school's teachers and staff.

> We socialize together. We know the details of each other's lives. We notice what's happening with the other person. That's a pretty nontraditional way of being an administrator because administrators are routinely advised not to make friends with the staff.

Sarah goes on to explain why this advice is given: "Then, when . . . you have to reprimand somebody or something, it's all the more difficult."

Still, Sarah believes that building friendships and a sense of community is worth the effort. "The benefits that you get back are amazing." One of the benefits is the creation of a strong sense of support and caring among teachers, parents, and children at Greene Elementary. "I don't think you can have a larger school community if your staff isn't a community," explains Sarah. "The staff has to . . . walk its talk. If we haven't developed that among ourselves, we can't expect to have that happen around us."

One of the personal benefits of this sense of community for Sarah has been the response of the staff to her and her partner, Joan. Joan attends many school functions with Sarah, and they have been accepted along with the families of other staff members. Sarah says she thinks the staff is proud of their ability to accept her lifestyle. Although she is aware that at any time, the larger community of the district and city could "make good use" of the possibility that she is a lesbian, the school community remains close and supportive.

This is not to say that building a school community was a happy, easy, Pollyanna sort of experience for Sarah. While some teachers were gradually bonding and becoming a trusting community in the school, others were leaving. Sarah says she was

> clear about what I stood for and the kind of learning environment I could imagine for the school. The people for whom this vision was outside their comfort zone began to pick fights, to skirmish, and go around talking about me or what I was trying to do. Conflict with them would escalate. I didn't necessarily

take them on, but I didn't change my position, either. Some teachers elected to transfer. That was really easy. They just said, "We can't do this anymore. We're going to go somewhere else," and they would go.

Although Sarah describes this as easy, these were hard times for her. "They would often go, leaving a mess behind them," she explains.

> For instance, they would complain to my boss about my behavior, about how I was creating an inside and an outside group. Then, I would get called on the carpet, and I would probably have something written up in my evaluation about how I wasn't doing a good job with staff relations.

At this point, Sarah can see that even with the problems for her, their leaving was helpful to her efforts to build a community of strong teachers. "One by one, they left," she says, "and I would almost always learn after they were gone that it was the right thing. For example, one of them who left was bruising and hurting children in the classroom." Another teacher was strongly encouraged to retire by Sarah. "I said, 'Look, if you don't retire, you're on a plan of assistance next year.' " After he left, Sarah discovered that he had pleaded no contest to a case of indecent exposure on an elementary school playground several years beforehand. "This is what we're talking about," Sarah explains. "We're not talking about good people who just happen to have a philosophical difference." When she reflects on how these situations looked to the community and the district, she feels that "it's really misunderstood when you look at all this from the outside."

Deciding Not to Be Crazy

Sarah describes herself as a "classic resilient kid." Born prematurely and weighing only four pounds, she came home needing to be fed frequently. An often-told family story involves her as a 6-week-old infant, crying in her crib. Her father brags that he went into her bedroom and "spanked" her until she stopped crying. This began a life of constant emotional and physical abuse for Sarah. Her father, addicted to alcohol and to drugs that were easily available to him as a physician, would beat her until she could barely stand. After one of these episodes, Sarah remembers her father sending her into the living room to apologize to her mother. When Sarah wobbled into the room and said, "I'm sorry," her mother looked up from her desk and then back down without a word.

Sarah's brother, 14 months younger than she, was never touched. The house was flooded with photos of him and only one or two of Sarah. Her father punished her, he said, so she would not be like his mother. "Ironically," Sarah says, "I think I am a lot like her."

Sarah coped with her life by frequently living in a fantasy world, creating places that were safe and happy for her. By age 9, she was living almost constantly in her fantasies, returning less and less frequently to the "real world." She remembers a particular day, as she was walking down the street, lost in her fantasies, when she thought, "I have to stop doing this. If I don't, I'll be crazy." She began to discipline herself to "say the truth as best I could." She says it was the hardest thing she's ever had to do.

Now, Sarah feels that giving care to the children in her school is partly a way for her to "remake my childhood over and over." With a PhD in English, Sarah is conscious that she carries her father's title of "Doctor." When I asked her what that meant to her, she replied, "Sometimes, I think I can undo some of the harm he's done."

The place where Sarah is presently undoing that harm is Greene Elementary School. As a "doctor," she works her own cures on the children through her tireless efforts and the innovative programs she has created. Because of her background, Sarah describes Greene School as a "wonderful fit." The sense of community in the school and the surrounding neighborhood is similar to the sense of community Sarah felt growing up in a small town where she had friends from all classes of people. Her grandparents were farmers, and although she now lives and works in a large city, she believes that small towns are recreated in large cities. Communities form within city neighborhoods, this one familiar in its problems: drug abuse, physical abuse, sexual abuse—problems Sarah knows firsthand. She says of the Greene School community, "I know these people. I have witnessed their lives before." I can't help thinking how fortunate the teachers, parents, and students of Greene Elementary are that Sarah now stands as a witness to their present lives and as a powerful force making a difference in all the lives she touches.

10

Being a Late Bloomer

Tina's Story—
A Filipina Woman

*A young boy in my garden is bailing out water from his
flower patch. When I ask him why he tells me young seeds
that have not seen the sun forget and drown easily.*

—Audre Lorde (1978b), "Coping"

Tina is today a very successful educator who has moved up through
the ranks of the state Department of Education from teacher to principal to staff developer in the Central Office. She is respected by her
colleagues and is known for her thoughtful, caring, and intelligent
responses to problems she encounters. Being a teacher had been her
dream from when she was "a little bitty kid." As an elementary student, Tina loved school, played school when she came home, "made
like I was the teacher, you know, read books on the side." However,
Tina's dream began to look impossible when, as a high school freshman, she was mistakenly tracked into the second lowest class in the
school.

I remember very vividly going to one of the classes and looking
at the textbook. It was a very thin book and the letters were in

really large print. It looked like it was written for a blind person, and I remember tears and it was just . . . I learned nothing in high school. That's when I thought, "Well, maybe I cannot be a teacher."

The devastating experiences of her high school years left scars of doubt about whether Tina could ever reach her dream. Being tracked into one of the lowest classes

lived within me for a really, really long time. . . . I think it really hurt me. For the longest time, I felt that, well, maybe I cannot do this and I cannot do that, and every once in a while when trying something new, I'll have this feeling of, "maybe you're not good enough."

When she became a principal, she felt it was her

chance to make some kind of difference. . . . Here were kids who were from low-income families, many of them from families that were not intact. I really felt they needed to have the opportunities. It couldn't be, like my high school, where I knew I didn't have opportunities. . . . In fact, in my senior year, they said, "You really want to go to the university?" and I said, "Yes." All the other classes, the average and above average, were taking a field trip to the university, to do a visitation. They told me I had to take the bus and do my visitation alone because no one in my group was interested in going to a university. So that's when I really had my doubts.

Despite the difficulties, Tina went alone on the bus to visit the university. "I joined another group that was there. . . . Now, when I think about it . . . I must have really wanted to go. . . . And then of course, I was just very surprised that I got accepted."

Her university experiences helped to dispel Tina's doubts about herself. She met education professors her freshman year "that felt that I was smart. You know they would return my papers, and I would get A's and, 'Wow!' "

I would go to their offices and they would talk to me and they really thought that I had potential. . . . I really felt I wasn't smart, and that kind of gave me confidence that I could do the work and then after that I was OK.

Tina went on to get a master's degree in education and to become a very talented classroom teacher. Her early memories of elementary school had influenced not only her desire to be a teacher but the way she taught. Her experiences in elementary school

> were always active. I don't remember sitting down more than 30 minutes at any one time in any of my classes. . . . We made a bakery and made papier-mâché donuts and sold them. We had a cash register . . . and I think that has influenced the way I teach because I've never really liked having a set time for math and a set time for language arts.

Tina's innovative teaching methods and her creativity moved her quickly from classroom teacher to math curriculum specialist at the district office. Despite her successes, to this day, Tina describes herself as "the dumb one in the family. . . . I'm really the odd person, who really didn't achieve, because the other two are achievers." Her brother is a judge and her sister is a CPA.

"When I was growing up, I was really a rebel," explains Tina,

> because I was that weird kid, the kid who couldn't achieve. I know my mom had a difficult time bringing me up. I always felt like she was the one, not my father, [that] was always comparing. She would tell me, "How come you can't be like your brother? Why can't you be president? Why can't you get awards?" and that kind of thing. I don't think she really knew she was saying that, and now as I'm getting closer to 50, I begin to understand the perspective of a mother a little more and it's OK. . . . I just laugh about it. You know, it's easier that way.

On Being Filipina

Reflecting on her role as a Filipina in educational leadership, Tina states that, "I think mainly, as a Filipino, people think that we're not intellectual, that we really don't have goals." In group settings, "It's just a feeling you get." She would often function as a recorder or simply a member rather than "the one in the limelight." "People often say, 'Filipinos, they have no ambition.' You feel that, you just feel that!"

Tina's role as principal defied the stereotype she described, even though she explained that she also lives that stereotype. Often, when someone asks her what she thinks, "I just tell them, 'Oh, I don't know.' " A friend, having observed Tina's interactions with other educational leaders, asked, "Why do you act like that, that you don't know? Why are you not telling them how much you do know?" Tina remarked,

> I had to think about that. Maybe it's too much trouble to show people that they're wrong. If they want to think that way, then that's OK. I don't need to show or prove to people that I read or that I have ideas.

Tina was unwilling to stick out or show off:

> If you want to know me better, then engage in conversation with me. If you're willing to take some time, then I'll share with you that I do know something. . . . If people are continually giving advice and making me feel as if I don't know, then I'll just listen. That's OK, too. If you really want to know me, then I'll share with you some of my ideas.

Speaking of her professional career in the state educational system, Tina states, "I just feel that there is a closed group or an elitist group that you can't just go in and say, 'Here I am.' My only way into it is through someone who knows who I am."

In addition to struggling with people's stereotypes of Filipinos, Tina has confronted differing expectations for males and females within the culture. If you're male, "it's OK to be a leader. You're expected to be smart and to lead. When I was going to school, only the males were your presidents or officers. There were very few females in that role." Having defied that stereotype in her own life, Tina now helps to train many women who aspire to be educational leaders. Reflecting on the current climate for women educational leaders, Tina explains, "I think the kinds of schools that we want now are really where women are considered leaders." To enter district- or state-level positions in the past, Tina believes that

> if you were female, you had to go through curriculum, and that's how I got there. It was through my strength in curriculum. The second year that I was at the district office, I moved to the personnel office, and that was the first time a female ever was a personnel specialist in all the history of the school district. So there are certain positions that are open to females, and I think in the past 4 years, . . . the district finally had a secondary principal who was female. Other than that, the leadership positions were given to males. . . . [Her school district] was one of the last ones in the state to do that.

When asked what advice Tina would give aspiring women leaders today, she said they "don't need advice. I think they do quite well. There are a lot of role models, for example." Reflecting on her own struggles, Tina explains, "I think my problems are within me, not me being female. It's me finding myself. . . . I think I am sensitive about being Filipino, but not so much a woman." In response to her own situation, Tina has tried to recognize other minority leaders that she encounters in her work: "I really try to connect with them, encourage them."

Despite her doubts and struggles, some colleagues have recognized Tina for her abilities and encouraged her. At an early point in her career, her boss had suggested that she apply for administrative training. "He had said one summer, 'I think you should go and try this, not because I'm trying to push you into a vice principalship but because it will open more doors for you." After the training, she stepped easily into a vice principalship, because "I had developed a reputation of being a curriculum person." So the principal and the district superintendent both recommended her, saying that she could "really do something with your curriculum." Thus, because of her fine reputation as an educator, Tina was "provided with a lot more opportunities." She went on to become an elementary principal, with a vision of providing the children with a "better education than they were getting." She also worked hard to encourage her teachers to work together. From there, Tina moved up the professional ladder to work in the district office, and today, she is one of the highest ranking Filipinos in the state educational system.

"I Am Just the Instrument"

When she talked about her new position at the district office, she said,

> You know, I'm supposed to have a vision of where I want to take this program. Yet it hasn't been so much where I want to take it . . . as the kind of feeling I want. I want people to own this program. I [am] just the instrument to move things along.

Displaying her belief in collaborative leadership practices, Tina stated that she was not necessarily interested in "changing the whole thing and having my dreams or my vision but [asking] collectively what we want the profession to be."

Dressed in a long maroon silk tunic, black skirt, and black high heels with gold bows on them, Tina is a study in grace and caring as she works with her colleagues. I watched her work all one morning planning a curriculum with three others. When the planning session was done, Tina noticed that the young secretaries in the office were eating lunch while holding their plates on their laps. She invited them to move to our table to be more comfortable, assuring them that we were through using it for our meeting. Then she stopped to help a woman run off the last of some copies she had asked for and made sure that everyone either had lunch plans or was included in our trip to a nearby restaurant.

Being very soft-spoken, Tina uses her large, dark eyes to say a lot of things not said aloud. When her colleague talked of how frustrated she was by two others who could not seem to get along, Tina listened quietly. "They make me want to smoke a cigarette," her colleague said, reaching for the peanut brittle on the table. Despite her quiet and accepting manner, Tina clearly is able to make her wishes known. A minute later, she softly chastised her colleague for putting a person on the program that Tina did not think would contribute much, mostly through the look she gave her. When her colleague asked, "Do you want me to take his name off the program?" Tina said no. "I think he would be hurt," she replied. "I don't want anybody hurt." When she found a mistake in the program they were discussing, Tina was quick to say, "It was my fault." One of her colleagues teased her, saying "You like to take the blame, don't you? I'm not saying it's anybody's fault."

The Power of Narrative

Throughout the planning session I observed, Tina emphasized her belief in the power of narrative as an educational tool. "I want their stories" she said, speaking of the veteran principals she works with, "because it gives you the context." Sometimes, the principals tend to lecture rather than to tell stories, so Tina asked her colleague, "Shall I say again, 'I want your stories?' " "No," was the reply, "because you didn't give them an example. They asked you again, 'Give us an example!!' " It was clear that Tina was reluctant to do this, wanting instead for them to come up with their own stories, not a carbon of what she might suggest. In a later meeting, she told a visiting teacher that the curriculum had changed; now, it was more problem based. She again explained that she wanted administrators' stories, "because they get at the context and attitudes of schools" in the state. Tina stated, too, that her students' stories taught her so much more "because it really showed what was important to them."

Tina not only collects the stories of others to understand them better but uses narrative or storytelling in her own professional work. One powerful story she has told and retold is called *The Starfish Thrower*. Tina wears a gold starfish with diamonds on it, given to her by her students. She said every year, she tells her teachers the starfish story and gives everyone small starfish pins as a reminder. The story tells of two people walking along the beach who encounter starfish thrown up onto the sand by the sea and dying on the beach. As they walk, one person leans over and picks up a starfish, throwing it back into the sea. The other asks, "What are you doing? There are so many of them. How can you hope to make a difference here?" The starfish thrower answers, "It makes a difference to that one!" Tina recalled that

the first time I really told the story was my first time at the district office, and I was going to talk to mentors of beginning teachers. . . . I think everyone had heard that story, but they were like, "Wow! We want to get out there and . . . ' "

"So," explained Tina, "I talked about the moral purpose of keeping those dreams alive because they were working with people who were just being inducted into the profession." Tina believes that for

teachers and for the people who come along, I think I have that moral obligation to help them see their hope, their dream of making a difference. . . . It reminds me that I need to keep trying to make the difference for them and in the same way . . . to [remind them] that they can make a difference

in the lives of the children they meet. At the end of that school year, Tina's students, who had remembered the story since the beginning of the year, gave her the gold starfish pin, thanking her for making a difference in their lives. Now she keeps it with her constantly, pinned to the strap of her purse, a visual sign of her philosophy.

Tina also showed me a book that meant a great deal to her, titled "The Precious Present," by Spencer Johnson. The story describes a young seeker who questions a wise old man about the secret of the precious present. The young man wants to know what the precious present is. Gradually, he realizes that the present he hopes to receive is really the gift of being in the present, rather than dwelling on the past or worrying about the future. "I think often we really don't live in the present and don't appreciate what's happening," Tina says.

I think . . . when you're younger, you're always talking of the future. In the past few years, I'm really beginning to enjoy the present and to think of all of my experiences and what I can learn from them. Whether it's positive or negative, I try to look for. . . , there's a lesson in there, you know? I do a lot more reflecting now.

Tina read the book about the precious present to her teachers when she left her principalship to go to the district office. She had started telling stories to her faculty during their meetings. She felt it was a more effective way to communicate her message than to lecture to them. "When I started a new year, instead of giving my message, I would read a story. . . . Speeches are not . . . it's not like telling them something. I often wonder if they really did hear what I said that first day." (Here, she laughs.) Tina felt that the teachers really listened more when she told them a story, "because there's a silence, you know at the end? People aren't shuffling papers. It almost creates a different room." It is in this newly created or transformed room that Tina is able to truly communicate who she is and what is important to her. Here Tina's belief in the potential of narrative is again underscored, that storytelling is a powerful vehicle for the creating of context, for unwrapping multiple layers of understanding, and for communicating her philosophy.

Part of that philosophy is her belief

that there are certain lessons that you need to learn in your lifetime. So I'm always looking for the lesson that I need to learn. I feel if I learn lessons along the way then I'll be a better person, a better human being, and I'll be more able to give back.

When asked about some of her most important lessons, Tina responded,

I think I'm really being tested to see if I can keep from making judgments. I'm still not good at it. I'm really working at it. I think I'm trying to learn how to respect myself . . . [which] is tied up with being Filipina. As a youngster I grew up in an Oriental neighborhood. We would play together, but I couldn't go into two families' homes because I was Filipina. In fact, when they saw us coming, my brother, my sister and myself, they would close the blinds and they would say, "Only she and she and she can come in, but you cannot come in. . . . So I knew very young that we were different. I still remember that. It was very hurtful. They used to call us names, too.

One family would not allow their children to speak to Tina and her brother and sister, even when they were outside playing in the neighborhood. Reflecting on those families now, Tina stated,

It is really funny, because now when we see them, they like to talk about my brother and knowing my brother. Sometimes, I wonder if people begin to like you because of your position and not because of who you are. . . . I'm real cautious in terms of what are people thinking.

An irony for Tina, given her past, is that people were suddenly eager to know her when she moved into a powerful position in the state department. "You know, when I took this job, people told me, 'Gee, Tina, you're going to have lots of friends now.' "

The loss of opportunities Tina felt as a young Filipina has strongly influenced her philosophy of education:

If we don't start giving kids opportunities when they are real young, then they will never have [them]. . . . To me, the elementary years are really important. . . . To some extent, I think the purpose of schooling is to perpetuate that democratic way of living, having opportunities. . . . The other thing I worry about is privatization, because I feel you'll end up with schools that are homogeneous rather than heterogeneous. The public schools will be for the middle or lower economic groups. You're not going to have that wonderful mix that democracy is built on. I think about whether we're really teaching democratic ideals in the schools. When you group kids by ability, I don't think you are doing that. A lot of practices communicate to students that not everyone is equal or will have equal opportunity.

One form of opportunity is embodied in the way educators teach, according to Tina. By grouping children according to ability and engaging in "narrow thinking in terms of what intelligence is, then we start treating students in that way," explains Tina. Even pedagogical methods can help or hinder this democratic agenda. If everything is taught

through lecture and through reading the book and doing the assignment at the end of the chapter, you take away opportunities for kids to learn in other ways. They feel they're stupid. They begin to think education isn't important because they're not successful at it.

Thus, constantly driven by her own experiences, Tina works hard to make a difference in the lives of public school children.

The Importance of Family

Tina's closeness to her family is another important part of who she is. Every year at Christmas, the entire family gathers to open presents: Tina and her husband and their two sons, her brother and his family, her sister and her family, and their parents. Before they open their presents, they gather for a family photo, an annual ritual. One year, her son gave her a clock with a picture frame in it containing two family photos, one from the last Christmas her dad was alive and the most recent Christmas photo. "So I guess the importance of family is rubbing off on our sons," she says.

Family has remained important to Tina. She and her brother and sister and their families gather every Sunday for dinner. With the strong support of her family, most especially her husband, Tina has been able to step from the uncertain young school girl she was into a more confident, powerful educational leader today. Despite the barriers and prejudice in her personal as well as her professional life, Tina does not seem bitter. In fact, her response seems to be a doubling of her efforts to be inclusive and caring of both other family members and her colleagues. Through it all, it is clear that Tina is first and foremost a wise and skilled teacher. She reads her audience closely, whether it be teachers in her school, students in her class, or colleagues in the state department of education. In describing how she tells a story to her teachers or students, she revealed that first she memorizes the story she wants to tell. Then she explained that she faces her audience and "I look at their eyes, and then I know how to tell the story."

Part 2

Concluding Thoughts

11

From Story to Insight

No one ever told us we had to study our lives, make of our lives a study, as if learning natural history or music, that we should begin with the simple exercises first and slowly go on trying the hard ones, practicing till strength and accuracy became one with the daring to leap into transcendence.

—Adrienne Rich (1978), "Transcendental Etude"
in *The Dream of a Common Language*

And in the belly of this story the rituals and the ceremony are still growing.

—Leslie Marmon Silko (1977), *Ceremony*

The previous narratives of nine very diverse women in many ways function as metaphors for their conceptions of school leadership. From the struggle for balance and wit, to taking a stance and not backing down, to weaving a web of school and community, to the creation of a sense of hope, to the resistance of the impetus to label and judge, these women's stories reveal profoundly new understandings of school leadership.

Margaret, for instance, strives to balance her home life with her professional life, mindful always of her duty to each. She is also aware of the many cultural differences between the people of India and the people of the United States. Here, she balances her own belief system with that of others, working to honor diversity and equity. She has rejected the caste system with its emphasis on skin color and has become committed to breaking the barriers between castes in India as well as working for integration here in the United States.

Catherine also works for equity and community, primarily because she has felt the sting of being dismissed as "an angry Hispanic woman" by her school district. Her response has been to weave a powerful web of school and community to support her work for all children. She has worked hard to develop her school as a neighborhood service center, writing grants and opening spaces for adult-family services. Catherine's own personal value system that honors the family rises from her Cuban roots as a young girl and the pain of separation from part of her family still in Cuba today. She believes in keeping cultural traditions and honors the diversity she sees in her own school's classrooms. Jolie, an African American woman, defines leadership through her own determination to take a stance for equity and justice and not to back down from that stance. Having been told "you're here because we're filling a quota," Jolie believes that leaders must speak with clarity, certainty, and authority. They must "confront head on those who doubt our intellectual capabilities because we're Black or Brown and women." For Jolie, leading is confrontational and "no-nonsense."

For Rachel, that resistance is nonconfrontational. Because of her Buddhist background and her Japanese American heritage, Rachel adheres to a view of the world as gray, not black and white. Her resistance to labels is as strong as Jolie's but much different in character and form. This resistance is more like water flowing over a rock, wearing it down. Yet whether these women see leadership as taking a stand or quietly wearing down their opponent, whether they resist by forming a web of community or using the wit to balance the diverse needs of others, all these women have formed conceptions of school leadership that arise directly from their own personal and professional histories. Their commitment to equity frequently arises from their own painful experiences of prejudice as children. Their response has been to redouble their efforts to "make the world safe for diversity," for every child entrusted to their care. Their ways of leading may be as diverse as their cultural heritages but all rise directly from their own complex social and cultural histories.

Just as some recent scholars have viewed research as the product of personal experience (see Neumann & Peterson, 1997), this volume examines leadership through the lens of personal experience, focusing on the intersection of the personal and the professional. We believe that viewing leadership through the context of individual lives yields a richer understanding of how leadership evolves and how leaders develop among minority women educators. We have drawn extensively on writings that portray reality as socially and personally constructed, on those who have begun to reflect on the autobiographical antecedents of their work as educators (see Bateson, 1994; Lightfoot, 1988) and on the works of Belenky et al. (1986), Caffarella (1992),Connelly and Clandinin (1990), bell hooks (1990, 1994b), Louden (1991), Nobel (1993), Pagano (1988), and Ruddick (1989).

The descriptions of women in school leadership that we have compiled here can be described as nested realities. Although the particular form of leadership these women both conceive of and enact is embedded in their personal experience, this experience is simultaneously embedded in particular social, historical, cultural, and economic milieux. Thus, they present both personal and contextualized understandings and images of school leadership that provide fresh approaches precisely because they have come from those with marginalized views. Their particularly unique social and cultural situations also provide us with clear glimpses of how personal experience influences both leadership philosophies and actions.

Four major themes run through these women's stories. We believe these themes will become worthwhile when, and if, they begin to create exciting, new dialogue that challenges traditional norms of school leadership, altering practice and adding, in significant new ways, to our current body of knowledge and understanding of educational leadership. A careful review of these women's stories brings to the surface sharp paradoxes that are, in actuality, continuities.

The first theme focuses on the fact that each woman has and continues to live with a sense of difference. Although each narrative is unique in its telling, the undersong of marginalization can be clearly recognized. Some were born in another country, some in the United States. Some carry skin or eyes of a different color or shape. All have faced discrimination or racism in some form in their lives. This continuous sense of difference pervades the ways in which they see and work with others. Being on the margins, for each of these women, has inspired them to "re"draw cultural, geographic, and institutional boundaries. Each, with her own color, history, and movement, has confronted and is confronting an archaic institutional paradigm of inequity, of linear and elite governance, and of devaluation of emotion and relationships (see Hayes, 1989; Tisdell, 1993). What is important about these women's lives is how each has forged her own identity against mass stereotypes that oppress, how they have established connectedness as a source of power and have challenged a hegemonic system. Each has defined school leadership through an ongoing conversation that reflects both cognitive learning, new forms of knowledge, and affective understandings that encourage a rediscovery of history and culture. A common response to these new understandings is renewed determination to make a difference in the lives of the children they serve. They work in various ways to create and sustain a sense of community in their schools and to foster both equity and justice as strong values within that community.

At first glance, this may seem to be a great irony: the women in this study, in so many ways, have felt like outsiders, yet they work so hard to create community. Is this a response to their own feelings of alienation and difference, or is it a recognition of the value other cultures place on connection and community? How can a woman who grew up in a boarding school in India have anything in common with an inner-city African American woman or a Japanese American woman from a rural sugar cane plantation in Hawaii? And yet, they do. They carry in their hearts the desire to create communities for children that foster a sense of inclusion and value rather than oppression and alienation. Each works to create a sense of mutual respect and connection. Whether in response to their own sense of isolation and difference or to honor the values of their ethnic communities, or both, these women struggle to respond to their own sense of difference in ways that work to heal fractured communities.

Perhaps the most stunning commentary is that the work they do to ensure that all children receive equal protection has been devalued as the "work that those people [of color] do and is not the work of the rest of us serious school administrators" (Jolie). This intolerant attitude fosters an accepted disposition of neglect that relieves mainstream teachers, administrators, and policymakers of their responsibility to "others." Struggling against institutional policies and powers that serve to cast these women in prescribed molds, the stories of each woman describe their tenacious refusal to be narrow, static, superficial, and generic. This action to "re"write the master narrative confronts a myth that rewards silence and conformity. Within the telling of these stories, the women express a political discourse of practice that reveals their disbelief that within their "heartland of American cities," the more "diversity or equity oriented" the political philosophy tends to be, the more apolitical the issue of diversity is (Catherine and Margaret). That is to say, the political textures are deeply subversive and oppressive regardless of public rhetoric to the contrary. For example, in the telling of family and cultural history, each woman expressed a fullness of security and comfort that led to meaningful connections. A different telling is used when the women spoke of the school institutions. Their language was often carefully constructed and at times underlined with deep waves of anger and frustration that suggested their inability to access necessary political socialization connections and "friends" in positions of power who could be helpful. In fact, when words such as *access to, barriers to, individual self-help,* and *individual responsibility* were used by the authors, the women were quick to ask us to define how we were using the terms. The concepts, they felt, had been politicized, as they were often used to stigmatize and separate people who pushed the institution to do something that enforced equity.

Furthermore, the women believed that it was not enough that an individual voice call for reform, as this does not, by itself, change social and political norms. To speak in liberal language as a single voice is politically modest and suggests that women school leaders of ethnic minority background have agreed to a social and political contract that encourages silence. However, to speak in a collective voice for a collective learning is a truly radical language that speaks of differentness and inequality. But it is this truly political voice that each woman recognizes as dangerous personal and professional territory.

Thus, we find a second theme emerging: Determination and courage lifts each woman's spirit. They bring enormous, sometimes dogged, energy as well as a tremendous sense of responsibility to their profession and their work as leaders. Often, their spirits must strive to soar against great odds, against a current of racism, sexism, and bureaucratic structures that privilege the few over the many. Somehow, they are able to struggle on against these odds. Yet their spirits manage to not just struggle but to soar against these currents. Although this requires enormous energy, these women have learned how to use that current to lift their wings rather than let it pull them down. Because they have crossed geographic and cultural boundaries throughout their lives, they have learned to navigate through differences. Each tells a story of self-identity that recognizes the multiplicity of self, that the one can be many. This belief dynamically links the self to family, cultural history, and communities of the past to the present, while it is simultaneously deeply concerned with future generations.

Jolie, for example, grapples with issues of gender and race, often finding that she must continually define herself to those around her. She tries always to be clear, she says, about "who I am and who I am not. . . . I am pretty no-nonsense, and I tell people this." "I try to develop a sense of hope every day," she says. Yet this is not an unrealistic, Pollyanna sort of an attitude. Opal, for instance, shared that "it's a matter of choosing after seeing the positive points, the negative points, and the interesting points." Firmly grounded in reality, these women nevertheless, understand the responsibilities they carry as leaders and continue to work toward their own positive sets of values and their own sense of who they are.

A third theme focuses on the ways in which their difference has instilled in these women a sense of compassion toward all children and a determination to help children to learn, grow, and overcome whatever obstacles are placed in their way. Their sense of equity and justice has been enhanced by their own experiences as minorities. Sarah, for instance, works tirelessly to "remake" her childhood, "over and over," in the children in her school. Opal underscores the need to make sure there is "time for each precious child" and Jackie seeks daily to make a "significant difference in the lives of her students." All these women attend carefully to the needs and rights of the children in their care. If there were only one compelling commitment that helps redefine the practice of school leadership today, that would be the personal power of "love." The women talk about love in a way that means respect, care, and responsibility without the semantic baggage (see also hooks, 1994b). It is a release from an objective language to a personal language about teaching, learning, and leading that empowers and accepts private and public activity of empathy and caring. Among the women who share their stories between the covers of this book, there is a commitment to the public process of loving, of behaving in a loving manner.

Love has not been the grist of academic dialogue, but we argue that it should be. Love is the foundation of each woman's spirit that has helped each to confront discrimination throughout life. Each woman has had to balance the ambiguity of a variety of often conflicting attitudes that have made her feel whole and at the same time fragmented, hopeful, and full of despair, mobile yet inert. Because of difference, each woman clearly recognizes that although her students are different from one another (and from her) due to culture, history, education, and family economics, they will all confront the ambivalence of attitude. As a minority woman school leader, each has had to learn (and continue to learn) how to encourage students and other professional educators to work through the paradoxical messages in life by placing a genuine love for children and for self at the center of her work (see also Gilligan, 1982; hooks, 1994b; Ladsen-Billings, 1994).

The interviews prompted each woman to reflect deeply on the meanings of their own philosophies of leadership and this notion of collective voice and collective learning. Each woman told of critical experiences that both broadened her professional knowledge and practical understanding of schooling and school leadership and deepened her aesthetic and emotive understanding of her activities. They described their work as school leaders as connecting the school with the children, their families, and neighborhoods and communities. They valued interpersonal relationships and the sharing of responsibility and decision making. Last, they questioned identifying only school administrators as leaders, suggesting that the commitment to care, to ensure equity and voice, is the activity of many others and that these others are the true school leaders. To many, school leadership was practiced by teachers who facilitated connections among children, between teachers and children, between the teachers and the parents, and between the teachers and their internal and external communities. School leadership is thus exercised by a group of committed parents, teachers, community members, and school administrators who work collaboratively around a set of issues that benefits students.

This brings us to our fourth theme, a recognition that these women have redefined power and authority in ways that equate power with connectedness, webbing their schools with people, institutions, ideas, and the larger environment. This new conception of power is both facilitative and caring. It is characterized by mutuality and synergy and is manifested through, rather than over, someone on the basis of trust and reciprocity (Dunlap & Goldman, 1991). Thus, it challenges traditional notions of bureaucracy, creating power through relationships between equals rather than as an act of domination within a hierarchy. Here, problem solving becomes more mutual and negotiated on the basis of reciprocal norms, decentralizing and enlarging decision-making processes. Individuals in this caring relationship are not rendered into other as object but are maintained and promoted as subject (Noddings, 1984). Both parties frequently benefit from this arrangement.

Much of the power these women have comes through these connections. Yvonne, for instance, who runs the first school of choice in her district, connects with the community, the school district, federal monies, city and state programs, state legislatures and policymakers, the mayor, and the local college president, all of which form a strong power base for her work. Jolie uses her connections to diverse populations and cultures around the world to forge a powerful self-identity full of feisty energy and resolve. "I can do anything," she says. Last, Sarah uses her strong bonds with teachers and the school community to support open dialogue through conflict and problem-solving processes. She says she is "a pretty nontraditional leader," one who has "never fallen into line easily." "I don't look dangerous," she says with a sweet smile, "but I am."

These strong connections are often used when these women pursue agendas that are acts of resistance to mainstream thought or ways of conducting business that these women find objectionable. They form connections both internal and external to the organization that provide them with the power base they need to pursue their goals. Like Sarah, they may not look dangerous, but their work clearly threatens the status quo. Sarah's efforts resulted in a complete turnaround for her school, transforming it from the district's dumping ground for screw-ups into an award-winning school with a national reputation. She believes teachers must be caregivers and nurturers and that classrooms must be communities—safe places where children can risk learning. Connections to one's sense of self also serve as a powerful base for action. Rachel, for instance, maintains firm connections to what she calls her own life-sense, quietly forging oppositions to the impetus of schools to control, to label, to fix things in black and white. As a Japanese American Buddhist, her efforts are silent but relentless. Margaret, too, finds her balance through self-empowerment. Like Rachel, she persists like water flowing over and wearing away at rock.

The ability to forge these kinds of powerful connections requires leaders who are extremely skilled in interpersonal relations. Connecting with others, whether they be legislators, parents, teachers, or students, is an art. It is through these connections that new pathways are charted, guiding their constituents into uncharted waters. They are always quick to credit those who have worked with them to explore new territory. Yvonne, for example, stated,

> I don't see myself as being central to other individuals' lives. I mean, I might be a piece, but I'm not central. . . . I understand my responsibility to [the school] and with it. It is a very collaborative, mutual vision and effort. It is dynamic and not static. I know that's a very different way to look at it. It's the Anglo worldview that you can freeze-frame life.

Likewise, Jolie's relationships with teachers, staff members, and parents reveal a strong sense of mutual trust. Even a teacher who had often disagreed with Jolie confided that they always sat down and talked over their conflicts and "always worked them out to the benefit of students. This is why I respect and trust Jolie."

Foster (1994) examines these themes of community and connectedness in light of the educational institution's atmosphere of isolation and alienation. Through these stories, we are reminded that the human story is a narrative of relationships, a need to connect with others and to build a sense of community. Both teachers and administrators have a moral responsibility to create a supportive learning environment that allows students not only to be independent by taking control of and making decisions about their own education and personal lives but also to learn to be interdependent by knowing how to communicate and work with others in a broader sociocultural community.

Elbaz (1991) notes that very little work regarding the moral aspects of teacher thinking exists (exceptions include Clark, 1990; Strike & Soltis, 1985; Tom, 1984). Furthermore, few works have examined the activity of minority school leaders who seek a just and equitable environment (Casey, 1993). The preceding women's stories are a strong testament for school leaders to champion the moral aspects of equity and fairness in schooling. Because each woman confronts injustice as both a female and a minority, she has learned that it wasn't one or the other characteristic that marginalized her, but that both, in concert, "pulled me down, like quicksand" (Jolie).

Making a Space for Learning and Growth

Many of the responses of these women to their roles as school leaders arise directly out of their own personal autobiographies. As minorities and as women, they are often doubly marginalized. Thus, many of their experiences in schools as children reflect the pain of being placed in the wrong track in high school (Tina), of being punished for coming from another country and therefore "different" (Catherine), of encounters with racism as a young African American student in a predominantly White Midwestern township (Jackie), and of physical abuse as a child (Sarah). These experiences seem to have renewed the determination of these women to provide equitable and caring schooling for all the children in their care. Many of them currently work tirelessly for educational equity in ways that are simultaneously caring of children and politically subversive. As women on the margins, yet with a clear sense of moral commitment to learning and the possibilities of schooling, these leaders' stories add to a current dialogue that values a capacity for empathy and caring (see Bolman & Deal, 1995; Dunlap & Schmuck, 1995; Sergiovanni, 1992), a need to develop connectedness through community (see McCaleb, 1994; Tierney, 1993), a commitment to personal responsibility and self-respect as well as responsibility and respect for others (Cohen, 1991; Fox, 1993; hooks, 1994b), and a strong testament for equity and fairness (see Casey, 1993).

The determination to provide spaces for learning and growth that were denied these women in their early years provides them with a compelling commitment that helps to redefine the practice of school leadership today. Astin and Leland (1991) observed this same passion for justice and equality coupled with a willingness to take risks in women leaders in higher education. Whether in higher education or K-12 public schooling, these women leaders' voices join a growing and powerful narrative that supports the growth of equity and community in education.

The Power of Narrative

The value of narrative is that, at its core, there is a living individual, not a commodity or capital. Narratives are rich in detail and situated in a history of human relationships that extends far beyond the teller's life span. It is this form of biographical narrative voice that reveals memories reflecting the strengths, weaknesses, and potential of the human soul, the complexities and contingencies of life decisions and actions, and the collective wisdom and naïveté of individuals.

Neil Postman (1995) underscores the importance of narrative in U.S. public education today. "Without a narrative," he writes, "life has no meaning. Without meaning, learning has no purpose. Without a purpose, schools are houses of detention, not attention" (p. 7). Postman asserts that shared narratives are central to the creation of "a public" or what our leaders would call "a community."

> The question is not, Does or doesn't public schooling create a public? The question is, What kind of public does it create? A conglomerate of self-indulgent consumers? Angry, soulless, directionless masses? Indifferent, confused citizens? Or a public imbued with confidence, a sense of purpose, a respect for learning, and tolerance? . . . The right answer depends on two things, and two things alone: the existence of shared narratives and the capacity of such narratives to provide an inspired reason for schooling. (p. 27)

We see an understanding of the importance of shared narratives, created through a sense of connection and community, in the line of leaders presented in this book. Shared narratives cannot be created without dialogue, and community cannot be created without a sense of inclusion and connection. These are the building blocks of shared narratives, the glue that helps create an inspired reason for schooling. Postman (1995) reviews a number of shared narratives, sifting through those that fail in search of one or ones that are "sustaining, with richness, seriousness and durability, the idea of a public school"

(p. 27). Some narratives that do not work, according to Postman, include technology, economic utility, and consumership. Schooling, he asserts, is not about getting jobs or being high tech. What then, might public schooling be about? The women leaders in this text have hit on one of the most powerful narratives suggested by Postman among those possibilities that lie "shining at the forefront," lurking "in the background, indistinct and half-forgotten," or "sleeping" and "recently awakened," all in "uneasy contradiction" to each other (p. 60). This narrative of schooling is the idea of diversity, which Postman describes as "a rich narrative around which to organize the schooling of the young" (p. 75). Having been excluded in many ways from the American dream, these minority leaders are passionate defenders of diversity and the possibilities for the creation of rich communities that it presents.

According to Postman (1995), this narrative holds both dangers and possibilities. He cautions against creating "a curriculum of revenge" (p. 75) in which previously excluded groups try to single themselves out for excessive praise and attention. As Cornell West (1993) has stressed, "We simply cannot enter the twenty-first century at each other's throats" (p. 159). The leaders in this text have not fallen prey to this possibility, working instead to honor diversity and opportunity for all. Postman concludes with a discussion of human beings as "word warriors" and "world makers" (p. 81). He asserts that "humans use language to transform the world and then, in turn, are transformed by their own invention" (p. 87). It is our hope that these narratives of minority women in school leadership can add to the richness of possible narratives in public education, both transforming the world of educational leadership while, in turn, being transformed by each other's lives and ideals.

References

Allen, P. G. (1986). *The sacred hoop: Recovering the feminine in American Indian traditions.* Boston: Beacon.

Angelou, M. (1993). *Wouldn't take nothing for my journey now.* New York: Random House.

Astin, H., & Leland, C. (1991). *Women of influence, women of vision.* San Francisco: Jossey-Bass.

Bateson, M. C. (1994). *Peripheral visions.* New York: HarperCollins.

Belenky, M., Clinchy, B., Goldberger, N., & Tarule, J. (1986). *Women's ways of knowing: The development of self, voice, and mind.* New York: Basic Books.

Bloom, L., & Munro, P. (1995). Conflicts of selves: Nonunitary subjectivity in women administrators' life history narratives. In J. A. Hatch & R. Wisniewski (Eds.), *Life history and narrative* (pp. 99-112). London: Falmer.

Bolman, L., & Deal, T. (1995). *Leading with soul: An uncommon journey of spirit.* San Francisco: Jossey-Bass.

Bruner, J. (1986). *Actual minds: Possible worlds.* Cambridge, MA: Harvard University Press.

Caffarella, R. S. (1992). *Psychosocial development of women* (Information Series No. 350). Columbus, OH: ERIC Clearinghouse on Adult, Career, and Vocational Education.

Carter, K. (1992). The place of story in research on teaching. *Educational Researcher, 22*(1), 5-12.

Casey, K. (1993). *I answer with my life: Life histories of women teachers working for social change.* New York: Routledge.

Cisneros, S. (1991). Bien pretty. In *Woman hollering creek and other stories* (pp. 137-165). New York: Vintage.

Clandinin, D. J., & Connelly, F. M. (1986). On the narrative method, personal philosophy, and narrative units in the story of teaching. *Journal of Research in Science Teaching, 23*(4), 293-310.

Clandinin, D. J., & Connelly, F. M. (1990). Story of experience and narrative inquiry. *Educational Researcher, 19*(5), 2-14.

Clark, C. M. (1990). The teacher and the taught: Moral transactions in the classroom. In J. Goodlad, R. Soder, & K. A. Sirotnik (Eds.), *The moral dimensions of teaching* (pp. 251-265). San Francisco: Jossey-Bass.

Cohen, R. M. (1991). *A lifetime of teaching: Portraits of five veteran high school teachers.* New York: Teachers College Press.

Coles, R. (1989). *The call of stories: Teaching and the moral imagination.* Boston: Houghton Mifflin.

Connelly, F. M., & Clandinin, D. J. (1990). Stories of experience and narrative inquiry. *Educational Researcher, 19*(5), 2-14.

Cooper, J. E. (1994). The metaphorical 'I': Journal keeping and self-image in administrative women. *Initiatives, 56*(1), 11-21.

Cooper, J., & Heck, R. (1995). Using narrative in the study of school administration. *International Journal of Qualitative Research in Education, 8*(2), 195-210.

Diamond, P. (1990). Recovering and reconstructing teachers' stories. *International Journal of Personal Construct Psychology, 3,* 63-76.

Dunlap, D., & Goldman, P. (1991). Rethinking power in schools. *Educational Administration Quarterly, 27*(1), 5-30.

Dunlap, D., & Schmuck, P. (Eds.). (1995). *Women leading in education.* Albany: State University of New York Press.

Easwaran, E. (Trans.). (1985). *The Bhagavad Gita.* Tomales, CA: Nilgiri.

Elbaz, F. (1990). Knowledge and discourse: The evolution of research on teacher thinking. In C. Day, P. Denicolo, & M. Pope (Eds.), *Insights into teachers' thinking and practice* (pp. 15-42). London: Falmer.

Elbaz, F. (1991). Research on teachers' knowledge: The evolution of a discourse. *Journal of Curriculum Studies, 21,* 1-19.

Estes, C. P. (1995). *Women who run with the wolves: Myths and stories of the wild woman archetype* (Chap. 16). New York: Ballantine.

Foster, M. (1992). African-American teachers and the politics of race. In K. Weiler (Ed.), *What schools can do: Critical pedagogy and practice.* Buffalo: State University of New York Press.

Foster, M. (1993). Self-portrait of Black teachers: Individual and collective struggles against racism. In D. McLaughlin & W. G. Tierney (Eds.), *Naming silenced lives: Personal narratives and the process of educational change* (pp. 155-175). New York: Routledge.

Foster, M. (1994). Urban African American teachers' views of organizational change: Speculation on the experiences of exemplary teachers. *Equity and Excellence in Education, 26*(3), 16-24.

Fox, M. (1993). *Radical reflections: Passionate opinions on teaching, learning, and living.* San Diego, CA: Harvest Original, Harcourt Brace.

Friere, P. (1970). *Pedagogy of the oppressed.* New York: Continuum.

Freire, P. (1985). *The politics of education: Culture, power, and liberation* (D. Macedo, Trans.). New York: Bergin & Garvey.

Gibran, K. (1951). *The prophet.* New York: Knopf. (Original work published in 1923)

Gilligan, C. (1982). *In a different voice.* Cambridge, MA: Harvard University Press.

Giroux, H. A. (1992). *Border crossings: Cultural workers and the politics of education.* New York: Routledge.

Goodson, I. (1995). The story so far: Personal knowledge and the political. *Qualitative Studies in Education, 8*(1), 89-98.

Grady, M. L., & O'Connell, P. A. (1993). Women in K-12 educational administration: A synthesis of dissertation research. *Journal of School Leadership, 3*(1), 39-51.

Gudmunsdottir, S. (1995). The narrative nature of pedagogical content knowledge. In H. McEwan and K. Egan (Eds.), *Narrative in teaching, learning and research* (pp. 24-39). New York: Teachers College Press.

Harjo, J. (1990). *In mad love and war.* Middletown, CT: Wesleyan University Press.

Hayes, E. (1989). Insights from women's experience for teaching and learning. *New Direction for Continuing Education, 43,* 55-66.

Heilbrun, C. G. (1988). *Writing a woman's life.* New York: Ballantine.

hooks, b. (1990). *Yearning: Race, gender, and culture politics.* Boston, MA: South End Press.

hooks, b. (1994a). *Outlaw culture: Resisting representations.* New York: Routledge.

hooks, b. (1994b). *Teaching to transgress: Education as the practice of freedom.* New York: Routledge.

Jackson, P. (1995). On the place of narrative in teaching. In H. McEwan and K. Egan (Eds.), *Narrative in teaching, learning and research* (pp. 3-24). New York: Teachers College Press.

Jalongo, M. (1992). Teachers' stories: Our ways of knowing. *Educational Leadership, 49*(7), 68-73.

Kelly, G. (1955). *The psychology of personal constructs.* New York: Norton Berger.

Krieger, S. (1991). *Social science and self: Personal essays on an art form.* New Brunswick, NJ: Rutgers University Press.

Ladsen-Billings, G. (1994). *The dreamkeepers: Successful teachers of African American children.* San Francisco: Jossey-Bass.

Lambert, L., Walker, D., Zimmerman, D., Cooper, J., Lambert, M., Gardner, M., & Slack, P. J. (1995). *The constructivist leader.* New York: Teachers College Press.

Lieblich, A., & Josselson, R. (Eds.). (1994). *Exploring identity and gender: The narrative study of lives.* Thousand Oaks, CA: Sage.

Lightfoot, S. L. (1988). *Balm in Gilead: Journal of a healer.* Reading, MA: Addison-Wesley.

Lorde, A. (1978a). A litany for survival. In *The black unicorn* (pp. 31-32). New York: Norton.

Lorde, A. (1978b). Coping. In *The black unicorn* (p. 45). New York: Norton.

Louden, W. (1991). *Understanding teaching: Continuity and change in teachers' knowledge.* New York: Teachers College Press.

Matthews, E. N. (1986). Women in educational administration: Support systems, career patterns, and job competencies (Doctoral dissertation). *Dissertation Abstracts International, 47,* 1138A.

Maynard, M., & Purvis, J. (Eds.). (1994). *Researching women's lives from a feminist perspective.* London: Taylor & Francis.

McCaleb, S. P. (1994). *Building communities of learners: A collaboration among teachers, students, families, and community.* New York: St. Martin's.

McEwan, H. (1992). Stories lives tell: Narrative and dialogue in education (book review). *American Journal of Education, 100*(3), 396-400.

McEwan, H., & Egan, K. (Eds.). (1995). *Narrative in teaching, learning, and research.* New York: Teachers College Press.

McLaughlin, D., & Tierney, W. G. (1993). *Naming silenced lives: Personal narratives and the process of educational change.* New York: Routledge.

Middleton, S. (1992). Developing a radical pedagogy. In I. F. Goodson (Ed.), *Studying teachers' lives* (pp. 18-50). London: Routledge.

Mora, P. (1993). *Nepantla: Essays from the land in the middle.* Albuquerque: University of New Mexico Press.

Neumann, A., & Peterson, P. (1997). *Women, research, and autobiography in education.* New York: Teachers College Press.

Nobel, B. P. (1993, August 15). The debate over la difference. *New York Times,* sec. 4, p. 6.

Noblit, G. W. (1993). Power and caring. *American Educational Research Journal, 30*(1), 23-38.

Noddings, N. (1984). *Caring: A feminine approach to ethics and moral education.* Berkeley and Los Angeles: University of California Press.

Ortiz, F. I. (1982). *Career patterns in education: Women, men, and minorities in public school administration.* New York: Praeger.

Pagano, J. (1988). Teaching women. *Educational Theory, 38,* 321-339.

Pagano, J. (1990). *Exiles and communities: Teaching in the patriarchal wilderness.* Albany: State University of New York Press.

Personal Narratives Group. (Eds.). (1989). *Interpreting women's lives: Feminist theory and personal narratives.* Bloomington: Indiana University Press.

Polkinghorne, D. (1988). *Narrative knowing and the human sciences.* New York: State University of New York Press.

Postman, N. (1995). *The end of education: Redefining the value of school.* New York: Knopf.

Reinharz, S. (1994). Feminist biography: The pains, the joys, the dilemmas. In A. Lieblich & R. Josselson (Eds.), *Exploring identity and gender: The narrative study of lives* (pp. 37-82). Thousand Oaks, CA: Sage.

Rich, A. (1978). *The dream of a common language.* New York: Norton.

Riley, M. W. (1988). *Sociological lives: Social changes and the life course* (Vol. 2). Newbury Park, CA: Sage.

Rosenau, D. M. (1992). *Post-modernism and the social sciences.* Princeton, NJ: Princeton University Press.

Rost, J. C. (1992). *Leadership for the twenty-first century.* Westport, CT: Praeger.

Ruddick, S. M. (1989). *Maternal thinking: Towards a politics of peace.* New York: Ballantine.

Sarbin, T. (1986). The narrative as a root metaphor for psychology. In T. R. Sarbin (Ed.), *Narrative psychology: The storied nature of human conduct* (pp 3-21). New York: Praeger.

Schmuck, P., Charters, W., & Carlson, R. (Eds.). (1981). *Educational policy and management: Sex differentials.* New York: Academic Press.

Schon, D. A. (1983). *The reflective practitioner: How professionals think in action.* New York: Basic Books.

Schon, D. A. (1991). *The reflective turn: Case studies in and on educational practice.* New York: Teachers College Press.

Sergiovanni, T. J. (1992). *Moral leadership: Getting to the heart of school improvement.* San Francisco: Jossey-Bass.

Sergiovanni, T. J. (1994). *Building community in schools.* San Francisco: Jossey-Bass.

Shakeshaft, C. (1989). *Women in educational administration.* Newbury Park, CA: Corwin.

Silko, L. M. (1977). *Ceremony.* New York: Viking.

Simonson, R., & Walker S. (1988). *Multicultural literacy.* St. Paul, MN: Graywolf.

Sleeter, C. E. (1992). *Keepers of the American dream: A study of staff development and multicultural education.* Washington, DC: Falmer.

Sleeter, C. E., & Grant, C. A. (1994). *Making choices for multicultural education: Five approaches to race, class, and gender* (2nd ed.). New York: Macmillan.

Strike, K., & Soltis, J. (1985). *The ethics of teaching.* New York: Teachers College Press.

Tierney, W. G. (1993). Self and identity in a postmodern world: A life story. In D. McLaughlin & W. G. Tierney (Eds.), *Naming silenced lives: Personal narratives and the process of educational change* (pp. 119-134). New York: Routledge.

Tisdell, E. J. (1993). Feminism and adult language. *New Direction for Adult and Continuing Education, 57,* 91-103.

Tom, A. (1984). *Teaching as a moral craft.* New York: Longman.

Tripp, D. (1994). Teachers' lives, critical incidents, and professional practice. *Qualitative Studies in Education, 7*(1), 65-76.

West, C. (1993). *Race matters.* New York: Vintage.

White, R. W. (1975). *Lives in progress* (3rd ed.). New York: Holt, Rinehart & Winston.

Witherell, C., & Noddings, N. (Eds.). (1991). *Stories lives tell: Narrative and dialogue in education.* New York: Teachers College Press.

Wood, D. R. (1992). Teaching narratives: A source for faculty development and evaluation. *Harvard Educational Review, 62*(4), 535-550.

CORWIN
PRESS

The Corwin Press logo—a raven striding across an open book— represents the happy union of courage and learning. We are a professional-level publisher of books and journals for K–12 educators, and we are committed to creating and providing resources that embody these qualities. Corwin's motto is "Success for All Learners."